TRACKS

IN

THE

SAND

TRACKS IN THE SAND

H. Turney McKnight

Illustrated by Inga Clough Falterman
Foreword by Tom Horton

Published by High Tide Books, Havre de Grace, Maryland

Edited and designed by Girl Friday Productions
www.girlfridayproductions.com

Cover & interior design: Rachel Marek
Editorial: Melody Moss, Ramona Gault
Book development: Devon Fredericksen
Production editorial: Laura Dailey
Illustrations: Inga Clough Falterman

ISBN (paperback): 978-1-7359210-0-6
ISBN (ebook): 978-1-7359210-1-3
Library of Congress Control Number: 2020921246

This book is dedicated to most of the people and all of the animals that appear in its pages.

CONTENTS

FOREWORD

This keenly observant book sketches a life lived well and authentically, ranging the planet yet rooted in the author's Chesapeake Bay and rural Maryland homeland. Turney will take you to some of the earth's finest skiing and to virgin Atlantic salmon rivers of the Russian Arctic, but equally he celebrates the riffles and marshes of Chesapeake rivers and the rituals of spring calving and summer haying on his Harford County farm.

"The smallest of boats and the highest of tides." I love that phrase from his essay "Messing About in April," because it shows a man who has learned the pleasures of being a part of his home nature, in an era where too many have grown apart. Turney could afford bigger boats, yet he has chosen to go small, befitting the Chesapeake's essential shallowness and its thousands of miles of land-water edges that are only explorable by those waterborne cognoscenti who reckon navigable depth in inches.

Fisherman, hunter, horseman, beef farmer, and quietly philanthropic of both art and nature, the author writes with equal delight about polo and pond hockey, of Hunt Cup banquets and dining more humbly (once was enough) on the flesh of snapping turtles.

Turney's pages recall some themes I always wished I'd expressed better in my own half century of writing about the natural world: *Citizenship.* Most take it in the narrow sense of civic duty, voting and showing up at the school board meeting and zoning hearing. But we need a fuller measure, an understanding of and obligation to the rest of nature. And that only comes from intimately inhabiting the places we're from. The life described here will give you a pretty good idea of how to undertake that vital task. *Owning land.* Companion to full citizenship, this is not a measure of how many acres one holds clear title to; rather it is from investing heavily in getting out afield and afloat, with rod and gun and binoculars and maybe, if you're so gifted, with the soul of a poet.

More practically, Turney's generosity has helped preserve some of the finest landscapes that I and many others have enjoyed though the years, from the quiet and untrammeled Eastern Shore creeks to Virginia's Atlantic seacoast. As well, from Smith Island to southern Maryland, from poetry and song to films and books, Turney has enabled artists who splendidly evoke the Chesapeake. He understands what writer Wallace Stegner called the "geography of hope," a view of place as more than its physical self, as an idea, spiritual and historical. "Tracks in the Sand," the signature essay of the book, is a lovely take on this.

Inevitable for those who share a life with animals and wild places, there's a lament for the passing of fine horses and faithful dogs, and for the despoliation of special places in our rapidly developing mid-Atlantic portion of America. But there's hope in every part of what might have been a maudlin final section, Friends Gone Too Soon. The passings here are about how to exit a life well lived, meeting death "with head held high."

Tom Horton
July 2020

PREFACE

Tracks in the sand disappear with time. Washed away, blown away, they are gone. Just as in the story which concludes the Hunting and Fishing section of this book, and which bears the book's title, we are left examining the few remaining physical clues, trying to discern what really happened.

What follows are some of my tracks through time. With the exception of that story, they are what really happened.

HTM
White Hall, Maryland
April 2020

I

PEOPLE, PLACES, AND PURPLE MARTINS

IDAHO

To my west, thirty-five miles distant, the summit of Oregon's 9,600-foot Eagle Cap towers in pure white majesty. Ahead of me, Idaho's Seven Devils range unfolds in the daunting splendor that severely challenged copper and gold miners a century ago. Eastward, the land falls away gradually to the valley of the Little Salmon River and then rises again to become the haze-enshrouded mountains of the River of No Return Wilderness.

From directly behind me: "CAN'T you see that these children are exhausted? WHY'D we have to come this way anyway? HOW much longer before lunch and a rest? WHY didn't we take that shortcut to the left?"

My wife, Liz. I was at seven thousand feet with her and our two young kids. Also sharing the dusty trail were our kids' two young friends, my old friend who lives in Idaho, a hired camp cook, and nine horses and mules, including the one packing lunch and the fishing rods.

We had, as a matter of fact, been in the saddle a long time and eaten a lot of dust. Liz was right. So we found a spot to stop for lunch by an abandoned miner's cabin. There, the breeze was refreshing and the shade was cool. Amid alpine scenery we stretched out on a lush carpet of grass and wildflowers and ate and napped. Revived, we rode on, and by midafternoon we were casting flies to hungry trout in a crystalline lake whose existence is known to only a few.

There had been many previous trips to Idaho, but never with kids this young. Once, in the days before we had children, we even took our dogs and so became the proud owners of the only terrier in Harford County, probably, that ever chased a bear down a scree slope.

My Idaho friend had suggested a somewhat tamer trip this time, but these were all really good, hardy kids, and I felt certain they would enjoy the extra challenges. Nonetheless, the previous winter I had in preparation taken a sixty-four-hour wilderness first aid course given on a remote and isolated Chesapeake island. The course lasted ten days and involved unimaginable discomforts, but it definitely made me feel better about heading out into the wilderness with these young 'uns.

We had traveled by rickety horse truck and battered Suburban from the flatlands of the Boise high desert to my friend's base camp at the edge of the Payette National Forest. Right away, we found that we didn't have enough pack animals to carry all our gear. So here's what we left behind at base camp for the rest of our trip:

- clean clothes
- foam mattresses
- enough soft drinks (out there they call it "pop")

Here's what didn't get left behind as we headed up the wooded and steep trail toward the high country:

- twenty-five-pound first aid kit
- beans
- vodka

Now at home this group of kids has trouble rationing the amount of time they stand in front of the refrigerator with its door open. To see them rationing their scanty supply of pop did the heart good. When a can fell out of my eight-year-old son's saddle bag and split open on a rock, it was a major catastrophe, but he took it stoically, like a man.

The horses and pack mules were great—surefooted, willing, and in good enough condition to carry us long distances in this rugged country. However, horses are horses (and mules are mules), and it wasn't until the kids had all been kicked, stomped, or bitten a time or two that they turned into really good hands. Liz was a good hand right from the start, of course, but it was still worth pausing to watch while she tried to put hobbles on her mustang at the end of the day. (If you go on a pack trip out west or a fox hunt in Ireland, never let on that you're a good rider or they'll put you on the craziest animal in the bunch, optimistic that you'll "make" the critter for them.)

One morning, we were sitting around camp drinking coffee, and I asked where the little girls were. "Oh, they're still out wrangling the stock," came the answer. Right, I thought, and a week from now they'll be back up in their rooms at home playing with their Breyer plastic horse toys.

The kids learned how to go to sleep on heavy saddle blankets instead of foam pads, lying on their backs and gazing up at the shooting stars that crisscrossed the sky. They learned how to soap up and rinse down in a mountain stream that gave you an ice cream headache just standing ankle deep in it. They learned never to get between the cook and his campfire. They learned that a man always takes care of his horse before he thinks about his own needs.

They learned how to ride to and catch fish in pristine lakes—lakes that stay remote for a reason. Most people's horses can't even make it to them. Figure seven hours of riding, followed by a quarter mile on foot through tangled brush you couldn't even get a dog to enter, followed by a slide down a rockfall and over a hornet's nest to water's edge. Once you get there, though, these high lakes tend to fall into two wonderful categories: absolutely teeming with medium to small trout or nicely populated with absolutely humongous trout. The fish in either category will take a fly readily most of the time. And it is not a question of delicate presentation and intricate hatch matching, either. Just put a size 12 Muddler Minnow over top of 'em, and you got yourself breakfast.

Those kids came out of that country weather-beaten and trail toughened. And they had earned the respect of the old mountaineer we met on the way down who couldn't believe that "you took them little buckaroos into the (name withheld to protect my fishin' holes) country!"

Yep, we did, and I bet the wilderness thereby won itself some excellent new lifelong friends.

THE HAY CREW

Midafternoon. Ninety-seven degrees. Humid. Airless. From horizon to horizon, a blue haze veils the broad valley of the Little Deer Creek, hangs hotly on its rolling pastures, its terraced croplands, and its woodlands standing like sentinels at streambed and ridgetop.

Behind the huge John Deere 4240 tractor the spectacle is stygian. A worker, only just visible through clouds of dust roiling from the pickup tines and belching from the chamber of the hay baler, stands on the wagon that tows behind. Sweat pours off him. You can scarcely tell where sun-reddened, grime-blackened skin ends and sodden clothes begin. His face is splotchy, his eyes sunken. He pulls a seventy-pound bale from the chute, presses it six tiers high, throws himself up after it, jams it into place, jumps down to the wagon floor, slumps face-in to the stack, head hanging. The job is too big for one man, but his partner had to leave earlier. At this moment, both of us hate his guts. Another bale slams up the chute. The worker turns and drives his hay hook into it, drags it back to the base of the stack, and throws it to the top of the load.

He's sixteen years old and in good shape. He'll be fine. Probably he'll be playing street hockey with Phillip a couple of hours from now. I'm proud of him. He's got a bright future. We've "graduated" nearly twenty summers of hay crews now, and the boys who've worked like this when they had to, digging in without self-pity when the work got inhuman, have turned out the best.

One, a husky, good-humored lad from a well-to-do family, became a tobacco-chewing, three-varsity-letter man when he went back to Gilman that September. (Do not read this as an endorsement for chewing tobacco.) One went off to New York to pursue an acting career and ended up marrying a famous congressman's daughter. Another grew up and became an architect but kept coming back to the hay crew when I needed him until, I guess, his wife or his firm's managing partner told him it was time to get a life. One's an MBA in Boston. Another a lawyer in Atlanta. Two are successful accountants, one a veterinary student, another a prison security systems specialist. Several were the first ever in their family to earn advanced degrees. All showed, under the hot June till September sun, the right stuff.

They could have flipped burgers or worked construction or even gotten some type of white-collar internship, but something drew these particular boys to spend their summers on the farm. Maybe it was because hay crew gave them a sense of real physical accomplishment, something a kid that age might not experience that often. At the end of the afternoon a boy can look at two or three extended-bed hay wagons stacked with 175 bales each to the size of rolling three-story buildings and parked on the edge of a fifteen-acre field where not even a wisp of hay remains and know that he, maybe singlehandedly, has put behind him a big, big piece of work. It's just not the same passing milkshakes out a window and saying, "Have a nice day."

With most of them, I think, there was another, deeper reason why they came back to the farm year after year. As they worked, tucked away in that peaceful and secluded valley farmed for generations by Kirkwoods, Andersons, and Smiths, these boys were in touch with some agrarian spirit flowing deep within them, a rural birthright that growing up would deny them. All were better men for it.

After the first hay cutting in the barn—five or six very tough weeks hopefully ending by the Fourth of July—sometimes we might take one or two of the crew with us to the beach or even the mountains of Yellow Pine, Idaho. Many of these boys ended up being like family. Speaking of which, Liz once said, "I dread the day my baby Phillip has to ride that hay wagon."

I'm not worried.

SEVERE WEATHER

I had spent the night in Northampton County on Virginia's Eastern Shore and needed to cross the Chesapeake Bay Bridge-Tunnel to get to an early appointment in the Norfolk area. The radio said a severe storm warning had been issued for the mouth of the Bay, and as I approached the northern end of the Bridge-Tunnel, a mile-long line of tractor trailers parked along the side of Route 13 indicated restricted traffic on the span. Nonetheless, my car was allowed to proceed on the 17.6-mile journey across the roadway a scant 30 feet above the surface of the water and through the two tunnels located at the major shipping fairways.

The wind shrieked incessantly, raking across the sea and covering its surface with great streaks of foam. The waves erupted from every direction in a mountainous chaos no small boat could have survived. At the rocks of the tunnel islands enormous geysers of spray gave towering witness to the fury of the forces unleashed. Off to the east, against the pitch-black bar of the storm, the lights of a huge ship disappeared and reappeared, never quite lining up horizontally.

I later learned that wind gusts of ninety-two miles per hour had been recorded at the south tunnel island, and that shortly after my passage the bridge was closed to all traffic. A trawler was lost off the Virginia coast that morning, and a rogue barge demolished the bridge between Nags Head and Hatteras.

Maybe I shouldn't have been out there. Do we overestimate our ability to master and tame nature? If man can build a bridge across the wide mouth of this mighty estuary and then drive across it in hurricane-force winds as easily as walking over to the salad bar, what in the world can possibly slow him up? As if to prove the point, a Plymouth Duster blew past me on Interstate 64, in a wall-of-water downpour, around a curve, at his "rightful" 55, at least. According to crash avoidance experts, a car will lose 20 percent to 30 percent of its reliable control on a pavement that is simply wet, and on sufficiently wet surfaces hydroplaning and *total* loss of control can occur at speeds as low as 30 miles per hour!

The storm I was driving through had been preceded by a "severe storm and coastal flooding" warning issued by the National Weather Service, one of three severe weather "watches" or "warnings" that recently occurred here in one eight-day period. (The other two were for a hurricane, which ended up veering away from our area, and a tornado, which struck us directly.)

The best way to receive such advance weather information is to buy a weather radio, costing $14 to $40 at RadioShack, or wherever [*author's note: Amazon did not exist when this was written!*], and tune it to channel 2 or 162.40 MHz. A severe weather "watch" means begin to monitor weather radio or other weather information sources closely and be *prepared* to take immediate action. A "warning" will describe the intensity of the extreme weather phenomenon—gale, storm, dangerous thunderstorm, hurricane, tornado, winter storm, etc.—the area to be affected, and the expected time of arrival. Where warranted, necessary precautions should then be taken immediately.

Our local weather band station, broadcasting continuously from BWI, provides, in addition to its severe weather warning function, an incredible amount of useful weather information for our immediate locality as well as for the entire region from the Appalachian Plateau to Downy O and the offshore waters, and for the interstate routes radiating from Baltimore in all directions. Hopefully my own weather radio will forecast some below-freezing weather in the weeks ahead so this writer can turn to the subject of . . . Pond Hockey!

POND HOCKEY

Straight out of the Arctic it comes, blasting across the great Canadian prairie, scouring our Upper Midwest, plunging the mountain towns of Western Pennsylvania into single digits, delivering finger-numbing, nose-running cold to our Chesapeake, pushing every last vestige of shirtsleeve weather all the way to the Azores. For a day and a night the wind blows relentlessly, thirty knots and higher. Then the second evening brings calm. On my pond, the suddenly still, super-chilled water freezes in an instant. Black ice! I give it most of the next day. By late afternoon, though, I've chopped a hole at pond's edge, made the mandatory thickness measurement, and I'm lacing up!

Long, gliding strokes. I'm a kid again! *Brrrruuuuuuppp*, a crack streaks across the ice faster than I'm skating. *Crrruuuukkk*, another one intersects it. That's normal, though. Just the ice settling. I hope. I slalom improbably through tall cattails at pond's edge, do a *geländesprung* over a pressure ridge, and skirt the certain doom of the outlet pipe. I get my hockey stick and a puck, shoot it across the ice. What's this? The puck sloshes through half an inch of water welling up from one of the cracks. Must be a warm springhead underneath. That's OK. It'll be ready tomorrow—tomorrow for sure.

They arrive as if they were summoned by ancient tribal drums. Hockey players. Each carries over his shoulder a battered stick or two and hoary old CCM Prolite Tackaberry skates. Shin pads are optional under sweatpants or over blue jeans. In the first group is the Old Guy.

He limps painfully from car to pond edge. On the ice, though, he is fast and aggressive, and he never stops smiling because on this hard, slippery medium he can cheat the old age that closes in. Unlike the others, his skates are saddle-soaped, blades oiled, too treasured to ever be allowed to rust. Off the ice, I run into him only every two or three years, here or there, but his eyes still twinkle, and they do so more brightly when they see me, for we are brothers of a hundred nights of pond hockey together.

Nothing is more fun. At its epicenter the game is fiercely played, at flat-out speed. At the periphery little girls skate in twos and threes, clinging to one another, and shriek and squeal when the action gets too close. There is none of the slashing, tripping, and fighting engaged in by our professional counterparts. It's not that we are gentlemen of higher character; it's just that paybacks are too easy and painful when you're wearing no pads. Also, the manly craving for good, hard physical contact is usually well satisfied by bone-jarring tumbles to the ice caused by cracks, pressure ridges, and debris of every sort, not to mention our own rustiness and lack of conditioning. This having been said, a goalie with a good eye and fast reflexes will sometimes make several quick stick saves in succession, and as offensive and defensive players cluster in the goal mouth with sticks jabbing and stabbing, it's just a matter of time before somebody calls for the but-terfly bandages.

The game contracts and expands, ebbs and flares up again, as groups of players depart and arrive. As night falls, cars are pulled for-ward and lights left on to illuminate the playing surface. A bonfire crackles at pond's edge. In its warming glow, prodigious amounts of hot chocolate and other reviving beverages are consumed. Finally, the last weary skaters return to their cars for the journey homeward. Left behind at the base of the waning fire, illuminated in its glow, lies a dark mixture of slush, soot, and mittens.

It is late afternoon. Withered leaves rustle in icy zephyrs. To the west, the sky is deep red; cold shadows lengthen. On the ice, a group of young boys is skating hard. One, my son, Phillip, the best by far, wears the yellow-and-black jersey of the Baltimore Youth Hockey program. The Old Guy is gone now, his skates saddle-soaped, oiled, and hung up in the basement for the last time. On the bench at ice's edge sits a new old guy. He has my skates. He is lacing up.

YOUTH HOCKEY

The road winds back, ten years in all,
Beneath cold skies, past town, past mall
From rink to rink, by night, by day.
Few words between us, a map to find the way.

To Twin Ponds, Skatium, Ice Gardens, Northwest.
To learn which team would be the best.
A team sport, aye, and there's the rub.
I worked full time, it seems, to help your club.

Did we attract and hold the very best?
No, I'm afraid I failed that test.
I apologize for this, but overall
Maybe we both learned more, the way the chips did fall.

Wissahickon, Wilkes-Barre, Chester County, Cabin John
Our road through time winds on and on.
Early mornings: Outside the rink pitch dark, hours till day,
But for me this joy: you were about to play.

You'll have your driver's license soon; this is the end.
I'll still be in the stands, but less as a father now, more as a friend.
So thank you for our hockey times together
And for the memories; I'll treasure them forever.

Your Dad

LIKE NOTHING
YOU HAVE EVER
SKIED BEFORE

I was on the James Bond Traverse, which runs to the top of the steep and narrow Alta Chute One, when I caught an outside edge and tumbled off the narrow track. I hit the snow a few feet downslope and almost immediately realized that I was in trouble, for I was sliding on my back and headfirst and picking up speed. I didn't know for sure what lay in my path, only that the traverse had been angling across and through a boulder-strewn pine forest. There seemed little room for optimism. My skull actually tingled in anticipation of the imminent crack against a rock. I struggled to get my feet pointed downhill, succeeding momentarily, but one ski was still on and it quickly flipped my head downhill again. Completely without control, I hurtled on. I hit a small ridge; my body tumbled; my remaining ski hit a tree and came off. I careened a few more feet and then came to rest on soft level snow. I was completely unhurt.

I remained there for a moment, mad at having surrendered all control to the mountain. It's not as if I hadn't been warned, though. When you step off the tram at the top of Rendezvous Mountain in Jackson Hole, Wyoming, the first thing you see in front of you is a large sign that says:

OUR MOUNTAIN IS LIKE NOTHING
YOU HAVE EVER SKIED BEFORE!

It is huge, with variable terrain from groomed slopes to dangerous cliff areas and dangerously variable weather and snow conditions. You must always exercise extreme caution. You could become lost. You could make a mistake and suffer personal injury or death. Protect yourself—understand the trail map and ask questions before you proceed. Obey all trail signs and markers. Please think and be careful.

GIVE THIS SPECIAL MOUNTAIN
THE RESPECT IT DESERVES!

Some people read this sign and climb right back into the tram for the return trip to the bottom, a drop of 4,139 vertical feet, which makes this the steepest ski mountain in America. For these folks, their first trip to Jackson Hole will probably be their last. "Surveys show that people are about as eager to come to Jackson Hole to ski a second time as they are to make a second trip to Rwanda," grumbles a local booster magazine. For sure, this is a mountain that quickly exposes skiers' weaknesses, and those who don't wish to be so exposed go elsewhere. But there are those who immensely enjoy it here and are fiercely loyal. Attuned to their spirit, the operators of the resort generally let these souls have their way to shred the mountain . . . or be shredded by it.

The resort does constantly monitor avalanche danger, and threatened areas are stabilized with explosives or closed. (Even so, avalanches happen, and people are caught and sometimes die—one woman was killed this year.) Also hidden perils such as cliffs are for the most part marked in some way. Other than that, the mountain is open. If you want to jump off a ledge (the only way) into the narrow, rock-wall-lined, forty-degree slope of Corbet's Couloir, you are welcome to. Watching from the lip while an expert and intrepid group from New Zealand did so was one of the high points of our trip. Their faces were tight with fear as they analyzed beforehand precisely where each turn would have to be carved if they were to avoid the fate of the *instructor* who recently broke a leg there or the *Olympic downhill racer* who fell the last time he went in and slid all the way to the bottom.

"Extreme" snowboarders and skiers can push their personal envelopes with leaps off the granite outcrops or powder runs down the steep backcountry bowls. The mountain has gotten into the blood of these people. They watch it and study it, constantly measuring it and seeking ways to measure themselves by it.

Brian, the ski bum, middle-aged like me, drives a truck in the summer to pay for his winter lift pass. His mind-boggling ski tracks were visible in the snow from near the top of Upper Sublette Ridge chair lift. "I was just watchin' and lookin'; every day I would study it and think about it. Watchin', lookin' some more; seemed like I just had to try it." On telemark skis he threaded through trees on a steep slope, plunged off a fifteen-foot ledge, landed on an even steeper slope, threaded more trees for a hundred feet or so, then soared off a sixty-foot rock face. People who watched said they were awed by how long he seemed to hang in the air before he landed, just clearing the bottom of the rock face. "Yeah, man, I could feel those rocks going by," he said while grinning. Everybody knew whose ski tracks they were. Brian ruled! For a while.

He was far from the only larger-than-life individual we met. Jackson Hole is a magnet for them, from all over the world, ski adventurers and outdoorsmen and women drawn together by the purity of the experience on this mountain. As Wallace Stegner suggested in his essay "The Rediscovery of America: 1946":

> Instead of thinking what men did to the mountains, he kept his mind on what the mountains did to men, and he might not have considered the [effects of men's use] too heavy a price for the health, the happiness, and eventually the cleansing of taste, that [men and women] derive from the Snowy Range.

There was Augie—August—a tram driver, as tall and elegant an individual as the name suggests. "Welcome to Jackson Hole. Expert skiers only recommended from the top of the tram. The visibility in Rendezvous Bowl today is . . . moderate. Skiers who endanger others can and will lose their lift passes. For those who wish, a tram for the bottom will depart roughly every twelve minutes. Thanks, and have a great time." And winsome Christine, mountain patrol and tram driver by day, cabaret singer in the evening. Beautiful Elisa from "back east," nurse in the clinic operating room, went four years watching the battered bodies being brought into her shop before she dared try the mountain; now expert skier. Tommy Moe, Olympic downhill winner getting back into shape on the mountain after an operation, signing his autograph with a grin, followed everywhere by a plume of youthful ski race wannabees.

Finally, Steve, our guide, instructor, humorist, and mountain philosopher. Off his skis he moved like the laboratory assistant in Mel Brooks's *Young Frankenstein.* Maybe his boots were just extra stiff. On skis the most technically perfect and powerful skier I have ever seen. "Last run now; muscle memory time. You're tired? Well let me tell you, the mountain doesn't care whether you're tired or not. The mountain won't cut you any slack 'cause you're tired." Or entering at the front of a lift line, "Mind if we work our way in here? It's America. It's a free country. You can say no if you want." "Who's Dick Hertz?" "Where's Mike Hunt?" Or to a somewhat out of control skier, "Hey! Watch out, dude; comin' in a little hot there, aren't you? Why don't you just go ahead. We're better off with fireballs like you ahead of us." "And we're better off with *******s like you BEHIND us," hisses the errant skier's buddy.

Safety conscious to a fault, even Steve stares and stares at the mountain . . . and wonders *if*: "See the shoulder of Cody Peak over there? See the headwall with the narrow couloir opening up into the lower bowl? I want to ski that. It scares me to death, though. You'd have to mark those two small pines really carefully. You need those to see where the cliff starts. I'd sure like to do it, though." All this while his wife recovers from major knee surgery from a previous family outing!

A new day. The weather crystal clear. Fresh snow overnight. We get on the 8:48, first tram of the day. The car is full. Telemarkers with climbing skins and backpacks heading into the back country. Mountain patrol, instructors with their parties, kids who work in Teton Village getting in a run or two before work. As the tram starts its 2.4-mile journey, all faces turn upward in happy anticipation. The tram drivers choose their own music, and Augie's selection is Rusted Root's "Send Me on My Way." As if it were drawn along by the song's insistent percussion, the car rises through the trees; the lilting melody is a perfect backdrop as we pass over the boulders and jutting crags of the continent's youngest (and still rising) mountain range. Then we are in bright sunlight. Ahead the whole dazzling and vast snow and rock panorama of the Teton Range. Below us, the new snow has erased the tracks of Brian's incredible descent. The mountain rules!

MESSING ABOUT IN APRIL

'Believe me, my young friend,' said the water rat solemnly, 'there is nothing—absolutely nothing—half so much worth doing as simply messing about in boats . . . Simply messing . . . Nothing seems really to matter. That's the charm of it . . . Whether you get away, or whether you don't, whether you arrive at your destination or whether you reach somewhere else, or whether you never get anywhere at all, you're always busy, and you never do anything in particular.'

—*The Wind in the Willows*, by Kenneth Grahame

And thus, on an April Sunday, my domestic duties done, like my cur dog Brewster on a full moon, I'm out the door and gone. *Anna Banana*, the queen of my fleet, a twenty-two-foot Grady-White, has been hauled for bottom painting, so I'm trailering my sixteen-foot jonboat, a glorified rowboat with a forty-horse Johnson, light enough to wrestle across a mudflat, the whole works painted more or less camo from my serious duck hunting days.

The first thing I notice on driving into the marina is that the tide is exceptionally high. A plan begins to form, a destination as per the first paragraph above. I launch the jonboat, buy a spare tankful of gas, and head out Seneca Creek.

Now Seneca Creek is a perfectly nice little Bay tributary, particularly if your taste runs to fully bulkheaded shorelines with shoulder-to-shoulder houses and docks. At its mouth, though, just beyond the coal-burning, soot-spewing power plant, is something wonderful. To the immediate north unfold 103 miles of pristine, virtually untouched shoreline, a length of Bay, river, and creek side preserved in its natural state that would just about equal the distance by boat all the way down the Bay and up the Wicomico River to Salisbury!

What you see, as you cruise in these waters, is roughly the same as what Captain John Smith saw, and this makes the experience quite special as far as the Bay as a whole is concerned. The owner, of course, is the United States Army, for these are the shores of the old Edgewood Arsenal and Aberdeen Proving Ground. The Army extracts certain concessions from us in return for enjoying all this beauty from the water. You can't land your boat at all anywhere, for one thing. For another, there are times when you're prohibited altogether from entering the military waters. All in all, though, the bargain is reasonable.

Exiting Seneca Creek, I come first to Carroll Island, one of my favorite spots, except that I usually have to stay anywhere from a hundred yards to half a mile away from land here due to extremely shallow water. Today, though, in the smallest of boats and with the highest of tides, I can poke along right next to the shoreline, stop to fish the tiny indentations, generally give the place a good checking out.

Now a new plan begins to form in my mind. I know an even more interesting place I'd like to explore close up. It's a distance away across open water, over four miles, but the Bay is flat calm, and I'm just about certain it's going to remain that way, so I head off to the east and Pooles Island.

A word of caution: exposed water is no place to be in a small boat in rough weather. Things can go from being uncomfortable to terrifying to tragic in a very short time. I listened to the marine weather before I ever decided to begin this odyssey, and I recheck on the handheld VHF radio periodically. I know how to read and interpret clouds and wind, and I keep an eye on the sky throughout the afternoon. A change of weather might instantly have changed my plans.

Pooles Island, a mile long and maturely forested, is a commanding landmark of the upper Bay. The island received its name from Captain

John Smith himself, who designated it Powell's Island after one of his fellow explorers in 1608. The island was farmed from colonial days until it was taken over by the Army in 1917. In fact, its crops and livestock were plundered by the British during the War of 1812.

There is a handsome lighthouse on the northwest corner of the island. This was constructed beginning in 1825 by a well-known lighthouse builder named John Donohoo. It remained in operation until 1939, using nine whale oil lamps at first and later a Fresnel lens twenty inches high.

The island has gotten smaller over the years and will continue to do so as the water level of the Bay slowly rises, but it is losing ground much more slowly than Bay islands to the south because it stands on a rocky foundation. The shallow rock shelf that surrounds it combined with numerous conspicuous notices at the shoreline proclaiming "Danger: Unexploded Ordnance!" keep boaters a healthy distance away.

Today, though, I have plenty of water, and I run right up close to the southern shore of the island. As I shut off the engine to fish a little bit I become aware of what you might call jungle noises. Loud *whhrrrr-pppings* and *flappings*. I look up to find a spectacular great blue heron rookery. There are dozens of huge nests high in the branches, with great birds flying this way and that through the trees in their agitation at my presence.

I start the engine and move slowly away up the shoreline, respecting the nesting herons' desire for isolation. Large, brilliantly white objects on the surface of the water far ahead become, as I draw closer, a flock of tundra swans, resting in this peaceful place on their way north to their subarctic breeding grounds. I don't disturb them. Paired ducks, mostly mallards, are found in every cove. Maybe they will have more luck nesting here than on the pond on my farm, where snapping turtles and foxes wipe out every last duckling. A flock of bluebills rises and turns in unison ahead of me.

This side of the island has several decaying Army watchtowers. The roof of each is adorned with an osprey's rough nest of large branches. As I pass one, I am insulted loudly from within. A bird rises from her nest. In the air she utters no sound. Her wingspan, white from below, must be six feet. I am treated to a display of eloquently threatening body language, which has me glancing around the boat for the wooden paddle, in case I have to club the great brute away. I move on, and she returns to her nest.

A bit farther, I can see, not far beyond a strip of sandy beach, a solitary grave marker. It bears the following poignant inscription:

IN MEMORY OF
CAPT. ELIJAH WILLIAMS
aged 24 years
who was lost in a
snowstorm Feb. 24, 1855
near Pooles Island.
His body was found June 14, 1855
and interred in this place.
Also to the memory of his brother
CAPT. JAMES WILLIAMS
aged 26 years
Lost with him at the same time:
his body has not been found.
No friendly hand did close their eyes.
They saw no tear, they heard no sighs,
but in the waves they lost their breath
And they endured a watery death.

On the opposite side of the island, in a deeply indented and well-sheltered cove, I spot the ruins of a farmhouse and outbuildings. Perhaps this was the home of the proprietor of the orchard that provided the particularly tasty Pooles Island peaches to Baltimore homes in the years before the Army took over.

As I leave this cove, a tremendous crash rocks my boat and kills the engine. Exploding unexploded ordnance? Not funny. No, just my lower unit smashing against an unseen boulder. Time to leave; the tide is starting to run out fast. I head back toward the mainland. On the way, though, I can't resist detouring to take a sport run over the "non-navigable" flats separating Carroll Island from Carroll Point. Now I know a shortcut for later on in the spring to the fish-rich grass beds of Dundee and Saltpeter Creeks.

The pleasures of small boats! And of messing around in April!

THE ISLANDS

I have a buddy named Rich, who keeps his boat down next to mine on Seneca Creek. Sometimes we'll sit on our decks and talk back and forth across to one another about places we've been on the Bay. "What's it like around Crisfield?" I asked him earlier this year. "What about the islands around there?" "Crisfield's great," he said. "Somers Cove Marina. One of the best. Deep water, plenty of slips, everything you need. Any place else down there, forget it. Water's too shallow, everywhere. And the islanders? About the nastiest people I've met on the whole Bay."

I looked on a chart. There was, to be sure, a lot of blue, which stands for shoal water, around the islands and mainland framing Tangier Sound. Likely anchorages? Sheltered gunkholes? Nope. We were planning to travel to the area for a field trip. My brother told me he was going to spend the night on his boat at Tangier Island on his way there. "Stay away," I said. "They'll cut your throat for sure!"

Not long after, we stood on the huge work deck of the *Lonicarol*, a forty-six-foot single-screw Detroit Diesel bearing the traditional work-boat lines of her Reedville, Virginia, origin but magnified in size so as to be seaworthy when run in the North Atlantic winter weather that sweeps into the crab-dredging grounds at the mouth of the Bay.

With us were educators from the Chesapeake Bay Foundation, gifted, dedicated naturalists whose knowledge of their subject matter is only exceeded by their love for it and delight in it, men for whom coming in for meals or bedtime from the boat, beach, or marsh is the day's only hardship.

At the helm of his boat was Captain Lonnie Moore from Tangier Island, a man among men by all island standards—the best crab dredger, boat docker, baseball pitcher, whatever. He has a beautiful wife, Carol, an equally beautiful daughter, Loni, and a mother-in-law who is so proud of him she can hardly contain herself (and who, we learned firsthand, can sure cook up some island food).

We learned, too, that Lonnie was very, very lucky to be there at all. Several weeks earlier, in late March, he had been checking the raw water discharge at the stern of the *Lonicarol* in the middle of Tangier Sound when he accidentally slipped and fell overboard.

His boat, forward gear still engaged, no one else aboard, moved gently, innocuously away from him. They found her eight miles away. As she receded, Lonnie confronted the utter hopelessness of his situation. There was no reason to expect another vessel to pass in this part of the Sound. As importantly, the water temperature was around fifty-five degrees, cold enough to kill in a couple of hours. Waves of despair mixed with soul-draining cold whispered, "Give up, sink down into the peace of the depths." Then Lonnie would summon a vision of Carol and daughter Loni and would find the strength to keep swimming. Many times this happened. Suddenly, another skipper sighted Lonnie's brightly colored hat from a distance. Lonnie remembers seeing the man leaning forward to wipe the fog from the inside of his boat windshield with his elbow and staring through in open-mouthed disbelief at Lonnie in the water.

Another four or five minutes would have finished him. As it was, they made Lonnie spend the night in the hospital at Crisfield. Then, when he returned to Tangier, the islanders held something like an old-fashioned revival in celebration of Lonnie's deliverance from the winter waters.

So it was a happy man who piloted the *Lonicarol*, with us aboard, pulling a crab scrape through island waters the chart showed as too shallow for navigation.

Beneath the surface lay the marine equivalent of a rainforest, such, we found, was the richness and diversity of life in these healthy eelgrass beds. "Picture," says William W. Warner in his Pulitzer Prize–winning *Beautiful Swimmers*, written about the area we were visiting, "what a three or four foot cube of eelgrass forest must look like underwater. The forest will teem with life at all levels: sluggish predators on the floor, maturing fish fry and hiding crustaceans in the luxurious mid-section, and darting minnows in the canopy." When we emptied the scrape on deck we had vivid confirmation. Crabs, mostly juveniles at this time of year, shrimp, minnows of every description, eels, pipefish, seahorses, and several types of worms all flapped and wiggled in the clumps of eelgrass before we threw them overboard. The larger species that prowl the bottom and edges of the eelgrass beds make this a fisherman's paradise. Spot, sea trout, speckled trout, striped bass, bluefish, flounder, and black and red drum are only a few of these.

These eelgrass beds are so incredibly healthy and productive because they are all bordered landward by vast, undisturbed areas of tidal marsh. We can "put a man on the moon," but we haven't been able to invent a more efficient filter system for nonpoint source nutrients, toxins, and sediments that we daily send toward the Bay than that which nature originally provided. A natural marshland will significantly eliminate these contaminants; a drained, filled, and bulkheaded shoreline yields barren waters. It makes you wonder why those whose livelihood directly depends on population growth wouldn't be the very strongest advocates of marshland preservation, when healthy marshlands are a cheap way to help the watershed absorb the ill effects of more people.

As much as 90 percent of the soft crabs consumed in the *entire* United States come from the eelgrass beds of Tangier Sound. Indeed, these rich waters were sustaining human life long before Captain John Smith "discovered" the region in 1608. If you know where to look you can find wavelets at the water's edge lapping at virtual veins of artifacts buried in the marshy banks of now-uninhabited islands. My son, Phillip, who surely must have his great-grandfather Pearce's eyes, found a museum-quality arrowhead matching the characteristics of those dating from as early as nine thousand years ago!

A month later, I am back. The wind blows small-craft-advisory strength, but the *Anna Banana* is totally snug and secure, nestled into a notch in the marshy bank on the lee side of tiny Spring Island. It is nine o'clock at night, and the closest lights come from Wenona on Deal Island, some seven miles distant. A peeler crab on a trout rig fishes the eelgrass astern of my boat with the ebbing tide. An Absolut is going down easy. Leftover pork roast from home last night is sizzling on the portable stove. Suddenly the rod butt cracks in its holder; the reel screams. I grab a flashlight in one hand, the landing net in the other. At home in the islands!

OF WEATHER, SAND,
AND WILD PLACES

Hurricanes form in tropical latitudes, usually during summer months. Packing winds anywhere from 75 to 200 miles per hour, their tracks occasionally take them into our region, often with disastrous results. Because of the vicious effect when a powerful hurricane scores a direct hit, and because of the apocalyptic nature of what *could* happen to our coastal cities should just the right combination of superpowerful storm and high tides occur, hurricanes get lots of publicity. They're given names at birth and tracked with precision in the media. Generally speaking, we're made very aware of hurricane doin's.

There's another important family of storms, however, that we inlanders may not be as familiar with. Storms of this second type have hammered away at the Delmarva coast, with major consequences, on three separate occasions since last hurricane season. These storms are referred to as cold-core, or extratropical storms, because they form in temperate latitudes. As a matter of fact, one of the favored places for their formation is the Cape Hatteras area off the Atlantic coast. Locally, they are frequently called nor'easters because of their prevailing wind direction.

Extratropical storms don't pack as much wind velocity as hurricanes, but on the other hand, their severest impacts are generally felt over a larger area (almost 2,000 miles wide as opposed to 300 to 450 miles), their movements and effects are harder to predict, and they can intensify from benign to deadly just as precipitously, if not more so. The winds from these huge storms may blow steadily over a vast expanse of sea, pushing the water into mountainous waves. When these waves hit the coast, the results are awe-inspiring.

Here is an example: Last summer I took the *Anna Banana* on a journey around Cape Charles and up the coast toward Indian River, Delaware, her final destination. There were thunderstorms forecast, so I brought my boat in from the ocean through Quinby Inlet, between Parramore and Hog, two of Virginia's barrier islands. I anchored for the night in a marshy creek on the back side of Parramore Island and watched a lightning show over Norfolk before turning in.

I was back in the barrier islands this summer. To my amazement, the little deepwater creek where I had anchored was gone. You could even make out the marsh grass from the banks of the former creek extending right out into the surf. Keep in mind that my creek was formerly on the interior, mainland-facing side of the island. It were as if an Ocean City bayside condo, with deepwater boat slip, suddenly became a beachfront condo, minus slip, with everything in between completely vanished!

This impressive change in the shape—and in the very location—of Parramore Island is primarily attributable to the effects of an extra-tropical storm last October 31. Another nor'easter struck higher up the coast January 4, bringing pictures to our TVs of beach house sun decks spilling their contents into an angry surf. A third storm the first week in May eroded a lot more beach and brought to an abrupt end a fishing trip I was on, thereby planting the seed for this article.

People nowadays are pretty savvy about the natural balance, or "dynamic equilibrium," of barrier islands, whether heavily developed Fenwick Island (Ocean City) or pristine Parramore. Most everybody realizes that dunes absorb the terrible energy of huge waves and protect interior regions from overwash. Most everybody understands that entire chains of barrier islands act as one system in which the natural adjustment to violent storms is the change of bottom profile of any particular beach as well as the lateral erosion and transport of sand along the beaches to new locations. People mostly are aware that an inevitable consequence of the slow rise of sea level is the march landward of all barrier islands. Most everybody knows, in other words, that everything we do to save our resort beaches—dune reconstruction, sand replenishment, groin building—is *doomed to failure*!

Fantastic, I say. At least we are all going into this with heads clear and eyes wide open. Now, *spend* that $10 million anyway on sand pumping and shaping projects. Argue, if you want, about which groups should bear what percentage of the cost, but go ahead and fix the beach. Here's why. It's like saying that dredging the ship channel into the Port of Baltimore is doomed to failure. Of course it is; the channel is bound to silt in all over again sooner or later. It takes a lot of money to keep digging it out. Nature extracts from us a payment for doing business as usual on our terms when she has something different in mind. So it is at the beach. The costly projects we employ to preserve the resort beaches are still the best and cheapest techniques we have to save what is there. And what is there—Ocean City—is important to the economy of Maryland and to the enjoyment and quality of life of Maryland citizens. Including the McKnights.

So you're not sold yet. Well, consider this: What are the alternatives to beach replenishment, dune nutrition, and so forth? Let's say we just give up, submit ourselves entirely, so to speak, to the ways of nature. Time passes, hurricanes and nor'easters work their will. Eventually, in all likelihood, the Atlantic waves will be breaking over a jagged and grotesque seawall made up of the concrete and steel remains of the Carousel, Golden Sands, Sheraton, et al. And here's the bad part: leaving it all behind, the ultimate nonrecyclable by-product of our lifestyle, we'll then have to go in search of new, virgin beaches to "stabilize."

Such beaches do exist nearby. Imagine yourself driving in one direction in your dune buggy at a steady sixty miles per hour for two hours along an impossibly broad, gently sloping, shell-strewn, completely unspoiled beach. A lot of sand, no? That's how much beach, interrupted here and there by numerous mostly small inlets, lies for the most part pristine, wild, and natural between Ocean City Inlet and Cape Charles, Virginia. But wait. Now for the good news. All that Atlantic beachfront, all those barrier islands with their migrating sands, their landward salt marshes and meandering creeks, some with ancient pine forests, all with extensive indigenous and migratory bird communities, *are off limits to development forever!*

The protected area begins with Maryland's Sinepuxent Bay Wildlife Management Area on Assateague Island to the north and continues southward all the way to the Eastern Shore of Virginia National Wildlife Refuge encompassing Fisherman Island and the tip of Cape Charles. The largest landowner, however—the owner of the centerpiece of this immense tract of Atlantic coastal wilderness—is the Nature Conservancy, and it calls its prize possession the Virginia Coast Reserve.

The Virginia Coast Reserve encompasses some fourteen islands, bay salt marshes, and mainland areas inshore of these totaling well over forty thousand acres. The vastness of these holdings, combined with the fact that most of the Virginia Eastern Shore has not been the subject of intense development (in fact the region was *losing* population until the mid-1980s), has enabled the Nature Conservancy to embark on a protection plan that will be a model for use in important wild areas elsewhere in the world.

The Conservancy calls what it is doing a "biosphere reserve." At the heart of this concept is the premise that mere protection of core wilderness areas is not enough, that it is necessary to layer the protection with buffer zones to ensure that the core is not eventually degraded. A secondary premise is that man and his activities, both economic and recreational, have a necessary place within the entire healthy system.

Thus it is that the Nature Conservancy has not only "stabilized" its barrier islands (by buying them and taking them off the market forever) but is working in partnership with individuals, businesses, and government in the buffer zone to maintain and stabilize traditional agricultural and seafood harvesting practices on an economically viable and sustainable basis, thereby creating powerful disincentives for any damaging future development.

The islands themselves will thus remain as they are—remote, storm-swept, ever-changing, unspoiled, and beautiful. Most are open to the public for day use, and I poke around them a few times a year in my jonboat, always wishing my visit was going to be longer. For me, though, and for all of us, just knowing that they will remain wild and untouched, and the home of wild and untouched creatures, forever, is as important as visiting there. Wallace Stegner hit the nail on the head: "We simply need that wild country available to us, even if we never do more than drive to its edge and look in. For it can be a means of reassuring ourselves of our sanity as creatures, a part of the geography of hope."

VARMINTS

The Earth First! movement urges some fundamental reevaluations of the way we relate to the natural world and offers us some alternative value systems and specific plans for action worth thinking about.

But these guys start to lose me when they go on about reintroducing something they call "charismatic megafauna" into places I frequent.

Know what they're talking about, what they'd like to see roaming around again out there? The grizzly bear, the gray wolf, the eastern panther. Things that *eat you.* The Earth First! eco-warriors say, "Becoming part of the natural community means becoming part of the food chain." I'm like, "Wait a minute!"

Once I was fishing chest deep in a river up north when a completely harmless black bear came along the shoreline and ate my lunch. That's enough becoming part of your natural community for me. I like everything about the concept that my kids can stray out of sight and not get devoured.

Guess I'll never make a worthy earth radical, at least when it comes to the Little Deer Creek valley where I live and the central Idaho mountains where I go to play, among other places. Megafauna-wise, what follows will have to suffice.

Travel with me back in time, about fifteen years. We lived here, where we live now, but we had no kids. Instead we had three dogs, Jack Russell terriers named Fred, Francis, and Littlefred.

Fred was an awesome dog with a heart as big as his muscled body; Francis was the jaunty, dignified female, always good company. Littlefred was their son, a gifted dog upon whom I accidentally dropped a hay bale when he was young, but who came back from (expensive) orthopedic surgery to prove himself sensational in the semiorganized terrier races that were just then sweeping the countryside.

My wife loved these three little dogs with all the unleashed maternal intensity a woman without children of her own yet is capable of. They more or less ate at the table, slept on the bed, and went everywhere with her.

When they weren't off hunting.

Any of you who has ever had Jack Russells could probably match my stories of digging the little demons out of groundhog holes at 2 a.m., of calling in the backhoe man on a Sunday to pull the grate off the driveway drain in order to free one of the trapped and yapping little beasts, of posting signs all over the neighborhood, only—after wretched days of concern and angst—to finally find the missing terrier in a trapper's snare, her body still, amazingly, full of life.

On summer evenings—come to think of it, maybe this is where we went wrong—we would sometimes take our dogs down to the old Port Covington grain terminal. There, in the shadow of the overhanging steel hull of an oceangoing bulk freighter, it was not uncommon for each terrier to kill forty or fifty rats. That's a cheap date you won't find written up in *Baltimore* magazine!

There were episodes, too, involving other prey, chiefly cats. These tales are too sordid for general audiences and cannot be told here.

It was against this general backdrop of tiny Terminator mayhem that I heard a commotion down in the woods one morning as I was working nearby. I didn't think much of it, didn't check it out. But I had an uneasy sense that something might be wrong when I found only one dog, Fred, back at the house at lunchtime. A thorough search and a lot of calling failed to turn up the missing Francis and Littlefred.

Later in the day, I took with me to search two boys who were working for me that summer. We went down to the woods to investigate the area from which the sounds of a disturbance had come. The Little Deer Creek runs through the woods there, and at one spot it is deep and wide, forming a natural swimming hole. We walked along the creek, inspecting its undercut banks, which looked like possible locations for animal dens.

We gazed at the banks; we gazed at the water. We saw nothing. Then my focus shifted, and I found myself able to see down—down far beneath the surface of the crystal clear and shimmering water.

"Come over here, boys," I said.

There, on the stream bottom in about three and a half feet of water, lying on their sides next to one another as if dozing before a winter fireplace, were Francis and Littlefred. I could even make out the identity of each dog from where I stood on the bank.

We'll never be absolutely sure what happened, but I've got a good idea. Raccoons live along that stretch of stream. Coon hunters were enjoying their sport there before I ever bought my farm, and they still do. There's two things about raccoons that I never knew before this, although if you look in most any field guide there they are. One: raccoons are ferocious fighters, particularly in defense of their young. Two: a raccoon will intentionally lure a dog into deep water, then get on his head and drown him.

If we had eastern panthers, we probably wouldn't have as many raccoons. They live in my hay barn and make a huge mess and scare the help. They carry rabies and a serious intestinal parasite for humans called *Baylisascaris* and God knows what else. The coon hunters can have 'em as far as I'm concerned. A dead raccoon by the roadside gets no sympathy from me.

Raccoon meat is supposed to be tasty, just like lamb they say, but I'd have to be close to starving to try it. There's another of our local varmints, though, that I once looked forward with great relish to trying as table fare for the first time.

I'm talking about snapping turtle, a very large freshwater species common to our locale and indeed to virtually the whole United States east of the Rockies.

I'd occasionally run into snapping turtles basking themselves in boggy spots on my farm, but out of mutual respect we'd always made a point of avoiding one another. Then one day several years ago a very nice neighbor gave me twenty-five semi-tame mallard ducks to put on my newly built pond. In due course these ducks started to produce eggs and then ducklings.

It was a proud moment for everybody when the pairs of mallard parents would lead their recently hatched broods off the island in the center of the pond for the first time. As the little convoys would set off across the water, I'd count the number of ducklings in each group. I'd count them again the next time I visited the pond.

To my surprise, the duckling count would gradually diminish. The convoys would get shorter and shorter.

In point of fact, no pair of mallards ever raised a single duckling to the stage where it was old enough to fly.

A neighboring farmer who has lived in this area all his life explained to me that snapping turtles were getting my ducklings. Indeed, he'd even seen an adult duck on his pond narrowly escape one such grisly grab from the deep.

I set out to trap the turtles out of my pond. I found out that it's not all that hard to trap them using a submerged, fox-sized Havahart live animal trap baited with a bluegill. In fact my trap was almost never empty when I checked it. The ducklings never stopped disappearing, either. Furthermore, I had to deal with each angry, newly live-trapped snapping turtle in turn on the banks of my pond. After a while, I just got tired of it and quit.

Not, however, before I learned that snapping turtles have a vicious, lunging strike and huge, powerful jaws capable of instantly mashing through something the thickness of a horse's pastern bone. Also, they are not that easy to actually kill.

I am always more careful now when horseback riding, particularly in the spring when snapping turtles are often seen moving up toward the headwaters of the smallest streams. I don't see why a turtle that felt threatened couldn't cripple a horse, although I have never heard of such a thing actually happening.

Snapping turtles are supposed to have meat that tastes like chicken, beef, lobster, veal, maybe other things, too. I had an old-time Maryland-type friend who knew how to do old-time Maryland-type stuff like cook snapping turtles, so I turned a particularly large one over to him.

He kept it almost a week, during which time I would periodically telephone him for status reports. Yesterday my turtle was aging. Today it's marinating. Tomorrow it'll be simmering. That type of thing. I imagined to myself all the various flavors being exquisitely developed. I looked hungrily forward to the big day.

Finally the much anticipated culinary triumph was ready. As I remember, it was delivered in a big opaque jar, which seemed to contain quite a bit of sliced—or, more accurately, shredded—meat along with a lot of juice and some other things.

The McKnights heated it up and dug in.

Now imagine, if you can, eating something with a taste and texture along the lines of a truck tire that has been shredded, seasoned, and simmered for a week. I bit down, but could not gnaw through. Something in the seasoning burned my tongue. I looked over at my wife, who seemed to be having a similar experience.

Varmints, I decided then and there, are no darned good for nothin'!

PURPLE MARTINS

I'm not much of a bird watcher, unless I'm watching 'em down the barrel of my Parker Reproduction 12 gauge with Brewster, a black Labrador, thumping the marsh with his tail nearby. I once had a rare sandhill crane on my place for several days before the line of cars parked along the road and people with binoculars mounted on tripods peering intently into my field tipped me off to the big doin's.

But on summer evenings I often flop down on my back on the lawn just to gaze up at the aerial acrobatics of my colony of purple martins. Above me I see F-14 Tomcats at full intercept wing geometry, Mirage 2000s in screaming Mach 2 turns, A-10 Thunderbolts locked into deadly dives, and Harrier IIs in flap transition to the hover mode.

As a sky show you can't beat it. And the real bonus comes as a result of the fact that the martins aren't any more fuel efficient than their huge, armored counterparts. Possessing fiercely high metabolisms and digestive processes, they are required to consume, on average, their own weight in flying insects every day.

That translates into, plus or minus, ten thousand bloodsucking pests per day that each bird, whose short, triangular beak opens into a wide scoop of doom for bugs, removes from the area around my house. The insects are either digested immediately by the hunting birds or pelletized in the sticky goo that coats the inside of their beaks and taken back to feed their young.

You can read about no-mosquito summer anchorages in lower Dorchester County, entire pest-free towns in the Midwest, completely bugless herds of cattle, all attributed to purple martins. They say purple martins will keep hawks away from your chickens. And drive off that annoying flock of crows nearby. I can't personally attest to all these things. But when the first white men landed in North America, they found the Native Americans trying to attract colonies of the birds to their villages. Even if all the purple martin lore is only half true, that's still more than enough reason to keep up the Native Americans' effort.

It is all the more ironic, then, that man should be one of the martins' only two important natural enemies. We have cleared away the dead trees that provide natural nesting sites. As, or more, important than this, we introduced the starling and the house sparrow from Europe, and both these birds are able to successfully displace martins from existing nest sites. Finally, our use of chemical insecticides and pesticides, whether on lawn, alfalfa field, or the general fogging they do some places, has been the downfall of many birds such as the martin, which either ingest the toxified bugs and keel over or starve slowly from the absence of their normal insect diet.

Another tremendous natural enemy of the martin is weather. Martins are the largest member of the swallow family—the birds that come back to San Juan Capistrano the same day every year. It's been said that the purple martin would no doubt return to our area the same day each year *if* the weather here was as predictable as the weather at San Juan Capistrano.

But it's not, and so the purple martin has somehow got to figure out, and figure out correctly, when amid the vagaries of our April weather there will be a sufficient, sustainable diet of flying insects about. My farm diary shows recent return dates as follows: 1987: April 14; 1988: April 8; 1989: April 4; 1990: April 6; 1991: Not yet!

A sudden, unseasonable, prolonged cold snap and Mr. Martin is a goner, for he's got to have those bugs and lots of them. A couple of days without is about as long as he can last.

Not to be gloomy. I can usually tell without looking that my colony is here in the spring, having traveled straight through from the rain-forest jungle of Brazil's mid-Amazon basin. The birds make a sound, as they chatter on the stoop of one of their houses, like a particularly musical babbling brook. And once I've heard the sound, all I have to do is look in the sky for confirmation, and there they are, arcing happily upward like so many Roman candles.

II

HORSES

AND

COWS

SPRING CALVING

The old cow stood seemingly alone in a remote corner of her pasture. She gazed at me warily, but there was no warning switch of her tail, for this moment was similar to others she and I had shared on the mornings of nine previous Marches. One ear was directed full upon me; the other, cocked downward and out, was a semaphore showing me the direction I should go next. As I moved slowly and quietly, the old cow, exhausted and famished from her ordeal, took a few voracious chomps of grass. And then I saw what I was looking for. Nestled under a small bush, tiny, curled up, and all but invisible in the grass, with bright dark eyes, big alert ears, and a shiny black head held high on an already strong little neck, was the old cow's four-hour-old treasure. "Well done, old girl," I said.

We plan our calving to start early in March, when the severest winter weather has usually passed, but there are still no flies. Equally important, the cows are still being fed hay in the field every day, where they can be easily counted and checked, for 5 percent to 10 percent of them will experience dystocia, or interruption of normal delivery due to improper presentation, calf too large for the birth canal, or whatever. Fortunately, depending on how rapidly we can help these, up to 80 percent will be saved.

Nor is this usually that difficult. A cow with dystocia as often as not seems to beg you to assist her. Dr. Rutledge and I pulled or winched out many a steaming heap, and most were up and nursing improbably soon.

One day, however, Dr. Rutledge was unavailable, and I couldn't locate any other veterinarian to help. So I asked Liz to come down to the pasture. "Oh God," she said, viewing the cow with quite a bit of stuck calf protruding. "What are we going to do?"

"We're going to rope the cow, throw her down, and pull out the calf," I said, taking a couple of practice twirls.

"We're gonna what?" she said.

"I'm good at this," I said. "I used to rope competitively out west."

To make a long story short, an hour later the three—or three and a half—of us were panting, lathered with sweat and raked by briars, having covered what seemed like miles of terrain, mostly deep mud, thick brambles, and down timber. The rope had missed the cow by inches, by a mile, by any way possible. I think finally Dr. Rutledge arrived to slip a loop over the grateful animal's head.

Another time, I was way too late. The calf had been overly large and had died still in utero a couple of days before. The cow was down. I was lying on the ground, braced against her hocks and pulling her tail aside, with Dr. Rutledge in turn lying braced against my leg and straining against me to push farther up inside to decapitate the calf, so it could be removed to save the cow. The odor was unbelievable. After an hour or so of this, everything had been accomplished, and the cow survived. Dr. Rutledge sent me a bill for thirty-seven dollars. Wherever you are, Doc, you sure earned your retirement. I figured out that day why your son Jimmy chose a career in law instead.

Once we had a cow down and unable by any means to get up. The weather was wet and freezing and getting worse all the time. Cover was about a mile away. So we rolled her into the front-end loader bucket of the tractor and tied her in place. Dwarfing the front of the tractor, she nevertheless reclined quite comfortably and looked ahead with keen interest as we proceeded at a good speed down Harford Creamery Road. The car of a somewhat inward-directed acquaintance approached from the other direction. It swept by without slowing, the driver's eyes fixed straight ahead, I guess, or glazed over altogether. Talk about your tunnel vision!

The finest day of the season is when I take Liz and the kids out to inspect the annual calf crop. The six-to-eight-week-old babies have been so busy growing strong bone and muscle that they haven't had time to weigh themselves down with an ounce of fat. They bolt this way and that with sheer exuberance. Racing up a small rise, they become weightless at the top and explode in joyous bucks. Here are four or five racing one another at top speed along the stream. There's two having a practice bullfight. Another trots fearlessly up to the truck, then skids to a stop as some ancient warning sounds. The sun beats down; winter has passed.

HEY, MAUDIE

"COME ON, COWS. COME OOOOOOOOOOOOOOOOONNNNN, COWWWWWS!"

"Hey, Maudie. Boss's calling."

"Yep, banging a bucket, too. Probably some of that prime sweet stock feed. Better hump our hides over there before it's all gone!"

"Well, will you just look at (puff) Madge? Running for that bucket of sweet stock like Boss's been keeping her in a dirt paddock all summer instead of his best pasture (puff). Check out the dropped udder on that (pant) hussy. Them things pointing straight at the ground. I think I hear Junior back in the woods."

"MOMMMM. MMMMMMOOMMMMMM!"

"That's him. I told Martin not to wander too far off with those older boys or he wouldn't be able to find me at snack time. MAAAAARRRRTIN, MAAARRRRTTTIN!" (Gasp, cough.)

"Here we are. Boss's got the good stuff, too. Get your head out of that pail, Madge. Time to let the big cow feed. I said OUT. Maybe this will make the message clearer." *Whap!* (Cough.)

"Boss's taking us through the double gates, Maudie. Now he's headed for the corral. Bet there's sweet stock aplenty in there. Looks like the others all got the message, too. Let's get moving and beat the crowd. (Puff, cough.)

"The only thing I don't like about this corral, Maudie, is it gets hot as the dickens in here this time of year, what with sixty or seventy of us all crowded together. Also, it's just a little too easy for McDonald, the new bull Mr. Grason brought over last week, to stick his nose where it's not wanted. This sweet stock feed is nice, though. Where's Boss?

"There he is, Maudie. Back down at the double gates. Trying to get Marigold and Marsha to bring their young 'uns through. Screws everything up if he can't get the whole herd in at once. That Marsha's hard-headed, though. I guaradamntee it. Will *not* bring her calf into the corral. Boss oughta forget the Mr. Nice Guy stuff and let her have a taste of the Old West.

"Now that I think of it, that don't work on Marsha, either, Maudie. Remember the time Boss was riding that half-crazy polo pony of his, Bartles, at full speed, I mean flat out, trying to get Marsha turned back toward the corral? She swerved in front of him and he couldn't help knocking her down and galloping right over the top of her. Should have killed all three of them. Marsha just got up, shook it off, and headed for the creek bed. Didn't let 'em bring young Mason across that year till November.

"Look, Maudie. Here's Boss's nice neighbor, Mr. Garnet, come to help out. It looks like him and Boss want us all to go through into the second corral. Guess today's the day. In a minute Boss'll stand in the gap and let us girls out and keep the kids in. Here we go. All right now (puff), let's go around where we can look in through the fence and see how everything goes. Hope Martin will be brave.

"Yep, today's the day all right. Here's Dr. Jim, Boss's veterinarian. You know who I mean, Maudie. Guy who looks like he might have played some college ball. Wait a minute! What's going on? Boss and Mr. Garnet are loading McDonald in the chute first. NO!

"Whew. Problem's at McDonald's other end. Look at him snorting and rattling that squeeze gate. Now they got a halter and nose tongs on him and his head lashed down. Boy, is he mad! Looks like he might have the beginnings of pink eye. Remember years ago when half the herd had it, Maudie? No fun, to put it mildly. Well! Will you look at Boss's son and that other kid crowding up close so they can see the needle go right into McDonald's eyeball? Little ghouls!

"Man! When Boss opened the gate, McDonald came out of there like they were giving something away down at the pond! Now comes the part some people don't like to watch. First Boss and Mr. Garnet will run about eight or ten calves into the chute. Then Boss walks in behind them and crowds them all the way to the front. That's the tricky part. Till you get them little suckers all squeezed together good, they'll just as soon kick you to pieces, run over and trample you, just generally make it hot for whoever's down on the chute floor with them. I remember Boss had kind of a cocky little know-it-all kid working for him one summer. Put him down there on the chute floor. That kid ended up running straight up the chute wall like a lizard to get away from those calves!

"Martin came in with the first group, Maudie. Now Boss's got him in a tail lock and a flank press. Here comes Doc. He's got two 12-cc syringes in one hand, a can of antibiotic spray in the other, and a scalpel clenched between his teeth. Zip! Pink eye/shipping fever immunization in the butt. Zap! Blackleg injection. Next, a simple surgical procedu—"

"MOMMMMMMMMMM!!! BAAWWWLLLLL!"

"—procedure. Finish off with some antibiotic spray and . . . all done. I'm proud of my boy, Maudie. They're letting him out. Here he is.

"It's OK, Martin. Stings for a little bit is all. We'll go down and stand in the pond and cool off in a minute.

"Look, Maudie. Boss is letting his boy go down into the chute. He's going to wrestle little Mitchell. He's got him, too. Says it's kind of like checking in lacrosse. Doc thinks that's a hoot. Pretty good for a ten-year-old!

"Looks like things are going pretty smoothly, and they're working on toward the last of the group. Will you look at Boss! There's the dirt and blood and sweat and disinfectant, and on top of that a couple of the nervous ones got him pretty good. He won't be welcome at the lunch table like that!

"And out of the chute comes calf number thirty-six. That's it, Maudie. The end. Doc's getting in his truck. Mr. Garnet's headed home. Just one more thing. Boss is picking up a bucket. He's handing it to his son. He's pointing to what's scattered around the floor of the chute. Says it's the traditional job of the youngest hand. Boy doesn't look happy, Maudie."

CLEANING THE
CATTLE SHED

The Little Deer Creek Valley where I live is still cattle country, as are plenty of other places in Harford and northern Baltimore Counties. Here, during a dry spell after a late winter thaw, when the monochrome landscape seems on the verge of erupting but nothing has happened yet, passers-through may experience firsthand an ancient rite of spring.

Layered tractor tracks running a hundred yards up the highway from a muddy farm lane might be the first sign. One comes upon unexplained scatterings of organic material in the roadway. A formerly pallid stubble field now sports rich black stripes. You don't need any of this evidence to know what is going on, however. Your nose has already told you that someone is cleaning out his cattle shed.

There's a lot more to this clean-out than just making headroom in the barn for Bossy, though on our place she and her forty-five sisters do tend to get kind of scrunched up against the rafters by the time March rolls around. When conditions are right, then, we'll run the skid loader and the eight and a half ton spreader a couple of days solid carrying a small mountain of manure to various places on the farm. That manure does immeasurable good. It can also, as we will see, do immeasurable harm.

A plant body is just like a human body in that the healthier it is, the more resistance it has to critters from outside that would harm it. As cow manure incorporates into the soil in which plants grow, its organic material breaks down and becomes a source of nitrogen, phosphorus, and potassium, nutrients that are essential to healthy plants. Further, the organic material itself is like a sponge that sops up rainwater, which otherwise would percolate right down through the sandy soil. This moisture is then available to plants on a slow release, as needed basis. For these reasons, manure is just about the perfect soil additive.

The anecdotal support for this from my own experience on the farm is powerful indeed. The following things really happened: Let's start with the alfalfa field. When I started growing alfalfa, I had to spray the first cutting with Furadan, or the weevils would just about halve it. I had to spray the second cutting with Cygon, or the leafhoppers would have left nothing worth cutting. You don't want to know what these pesticides can do to birds, animals, and fish. Over time, I built up the soil with manure, controlled erosion in various ways, and made sure the alfalfa plants were not lacking in nutrients. I haven't needed to spray anything on my alfalfa for about ten years.

Even more amazing, consider the following: An alfalfa field is not permanent. Over the life of the field, various native grasses such as fescue and orchard grass will gradually choke out the alfalfa plants until none are left. The process generally takes about seven years. One winter I spread manure fairly heavily on about half a field I was going to plant in alfalfa the following spring. The alfalfa planted there outlasted the alfalfa planted in the un-manured half by about two years!

The experience in my vegetable garden has been just as dramatic, more so, really, because the vegetable garden is so small compared to the alfalfa fields, and so I can really throw the manure to 'er. The garden is in a stream flood plain where you'd think the soil would be naturally rich, but when I first put the garden in, the soil would turn fine and granular after a few tillings, and cracks would appear on the surface after rain dried. When it came to worm, borer, beetle, aphid, and slug, I had every variety. I couldn't grow anything unless I kept a fresh dew of Malathion on everything. It used to drive my wife crazy. Now? You guessed it. Pesticide free. Not pest free, mind you, but just the same, the only thing I can't grow now, just fine, completely organically, is eggplant. That's all right. I didn't like eggplant parmesan all that much anyway.

You get the point. And if you, living where you do, can't find some kind of manure around to enrich your soil, you're not looking hard enough.

More needs to be said, however. We farmers read all about oil spills, chemical dumping, raw sewage discharges, and other ways people contaminate the waterways. We drive down a country road after a rainstorm and see the absolutely incredible volume of soil runoff from one small, new homesite. We don't want to hear how we're the source of the Chesapeake Bay's problems. We're the good guys, for gosh sake.

Yes and no. We have to be careful. If we put more nutrients into the soil than the plants are able to use, the excess percolates down into the groundwater over time and seeps its way to the Bay, with very bad effect. There, this surplus nitrogen and phosphorus that we have introduced into the water causes single cell plants, or phytoplankton, to proliferate wildly. These rapidly multiplying organisms in the water column in turn intercept light that would have reached beneficial sub-aquatic plants. The latter die off, and the Bay loses vital spawning and nursery grounds.

Furthermore, when all these phytoplankton die, their decomposition uses up oxygen dissolved in the water. This produces anoxic areas where nothing at all can live.

In the first paragraph, I referred to cleaning out the cattle shed as an ancient rite of spring. It's recent, though, compared to another very real—and very ancient—rite of spring, the spawning of many of the species that live in our Bay. No one wants man's recent rite of spring to be the instrument of destruction of nature's ancient one. Nor need it be. Just remember, in adding cow manure to your soil, as in all things, moderation is the key!

SERGEANT BARTLES, BALTIMORE POLICE DEPARTMENT (MOUNTED)

I used to have a polo pony named Bartles. Yes, I acquired him at the same time as another named James. Well, Bartles was almost white in color with a handsome head and intelligent eyes. He was big chested and heavily muscled and brave as a bull. There is a semilegal maneuver in polo called the "bump." Nobody wanted to be bumped by Bartles. He was mostly gentle and quiet, though. I think my kids could have ridden him, but I never tried that experiment.

At the speed our polo games were played when Bartles first came into my life, I could aim Bartles pretty well. As time went by, though, the games sped up. Bartles turned out to be plenty fast. Unfortunately, though, once he got a good head of steam up, I couldn't turn, stop, or slow him down. He was useless to our teammates and a lethal hazard to everybody to boot, even the umpires. No amount of iron in his mouth made Bartles better. In fact, you could say that the pain from all the prongs and chains and *embocaduras* only made him worse.

One day we were bolting up and down the Brandywine polo field in a medium goal match, Bartles's head in the air, eyes rolled back to the whites, mouth open with blood splattering from the sides, my forearm cramping up from trying to slow the brute down, narrowly missing collisions with everybody, when it dawned on me: *this is insane.* The only thing this horse is any good for is practicing my swing at the walk or working cattle in heavy cover. I can't afford such a specialized employee. Bartles has to go.

Now I have this friend who lives near me in White Hall. He's a Baltimore city mounted policeman. So I called him up and said, "Have I got a horse for you!" He came right away and got Bartles. I didn't hear anything from them for a while, and then one day my whole family and I get invited down to mounted police headquarters.

We are treated like royalty and given the grand tour; we hobnob with high officials. Phillip gets to sit in a police car and run the siren, the whole nine yards. It turns out that Bartles is their favorite horse. They are all fighting over who gets to ride him. Bartles was working the 4 p.m.-to-midnight shift then. I watched him march out onto the mean streets at dusk, big rubber shoes clopping the pavement, neck arched proudly, summons book slapping him on the flank. It was a proud moment, I can tell you.

Later I got a call saying, "Don't miss the Thanksgiving parade: Bartles is going to lead it!" But somebody in city government squelched that plan. They didn't want a *white* horse. Can you believe it?

I checked on Bartles again today. He's a professional. Not too long ago, a guy who'd robbed one of the shops in Lexington Market tried to escape on foot. Bartles spotted him three blocks away and still ran him down. Another time, Bartles's team came upon a bleeding gunshot victim at Pratt and Marketplace. A bystander had a description. It was only a matter of time before the suspect was collared over in Little Italy.

Maybe you have ambitions of a law enforcement career for somebody in your barn. Here's what you do: Call Sergeant Sharp at the mounted unit. If your candidate is a gelding, over five years old, in good health, and at least fifteen hands three inches, they'll pick him up and give him a sixty-day trial. You have to agree in writing to take him back if he flunks out. These officers love horses like you do, and they are good horsemen.

And you might get a chance to sit in a police car and switch on the siren!

Author's note: On June 15, 2020, the Baltimore City Council voted to close down the mounted unit, which had been in continuous operation for 130 years.

I'M GLAD
MY KIDS RIDE

My wife, Liz, and I both were amateur steeplechase jockeys. In point of fact, each of us was fortunate enough to win the Maryland Hunt Cup, just about the biggest thrill of either of our lives. It is hard to overstate how much that race means to someone who comes from around here and loves timber racing. I've been retired from riding races for nearly ten years now, yet something still grabs hold of me the week before the fourth Saturday in April and makes me act a little crazy.

We've got two kids, Phillip, age eleven, and Anna, age eight. With their genealogy I suppose there's a good chance that they'll pursue the Hunt Cup, too, one day. We'd be happy and proud if they did, but nonetheless I think my wife and I would be the last ones to insist on it.

We've been so very close to timber racing in general and the Hunt Cup in particular that we recognize all too well the single-mindedness of purpose required to succeed, the bitter disappointments lurking at every turn, and the injuries and pain almost certain to attend the effort. We can tell you firsthand about the voodoo, magic, and pure luck that finally come into play to propel your horse's nose, or the other man's, first across the finish line in that great race, and maybe this alone is reason enough not to drive our kids to do what we did. But whether there's a Hunt Cup in their future or not, still I'm very glad my kids ride.

Which they both do, very well. When Anna's butt touches down in the saddle, it's as if closing a circuit lighting up a 200-watt smile on her face. She rides with her mother's natural angularity and grace, and win or lose in the show ring, she just plain loves it.

Phillip has the same natural riding talent and style, except he uses the body of a little fullback, or an ice hockey defenseman, which he also happens to be. And be it fox hunting or polo, his heart is always on the other side of the jump or down the polo field, way ahead of the thankfully wonderful ponies he rides.

To succeed in their horse endeavors, my kids will have to learn to get the best not only out of themselves but also out of their mounts. In so doing they will learn patience and self-control; they will learn that they must blend kindness with firmness, for neither works without the other; they will learn always to put their horse's well-being before their own.

They will learn, as I did, other valuable lessons as well. I'll never forget the time when I was seventeen or eighteen and over in Ireland between college semesters. I had a horse who had already been safely around Aintree for his previous owner, but nonetheless, one cold morning we set out early to give him a school over the smaller hurdles to sharpen him up for something or other. I had arrived at that particular stage of my riding career when I thought I knew a lot more about how to jump than my horse did, and as we galloped up over the hurdles I was giving him all kinds of "help"—a boot in the ribs to make him lengthen his stride here, a grab in the mouth to make him shorten his stride there, and so on.

Well, the poor brute went from jumping poorly to refusing altogether. We'd arrive inside the wings and he'd flat stop. The trainer didn't say a word. He just motioned to the horse's "lad," who had ridden him out from the stables to the schooling field and was standing nearby, shivering wretchedly in his tattered coat and gum boots. The boy looked like a waif out of Dickens; his total riding experience was a few months.

The trainer threw him up on my horse. Gum boots shoved home in the stirrups, shreds of coat flannel flapping in the wind, clutching the mane for dear life, the boy proceeded to soar with the horse over hurdle after hurdle. No words were spoken. Lesson learned.

Enough with the character building! My kids will learn, too, that their partnership with horses will bring them a kind of reward no other association can ever yield. When a dumb creature reaches down inside himself through near-exhaustion and pain to give us a gift—the gift, as it often happens, of glory—we have no choice but to acknowledge some higher power than ourselves and give thanks. When Tong won the Hunt Cup for me, I'm pretty sure his tendon went approaching the nineteenth fence, but he somehow dealt with his pain while going down the hill over the twentieth and toward the water, and from there on just said, "Heck with it, I'm gonna do what it takes to win this," and did.

After we pulled up, I didn't wave my arms about in triumph; I leaned down and gave Tong a silent hug. As I later found out, someone took a photograph of that instant. We found the photo among the possessions of my late father-in-law, David Pearce, when he died. David was a former Hunt Cup rider and lifelong horseman in every sense, and I'll always believe he recognized that moment for what it was and could relate to it.

But what, you might ask, about the physical risk to my kids from riding? I admit they will be in a lot more danger from horse sports than almost any other sport they might choose. The statistical probability of serious injury, even death, is significant. Just when we horsemen begin to forget that and get all comfortable, something tragic always tends to happen to bring us back to reality.

I have two personal answers—rationalizations, I suppose—on the part of someone who, when it comes to his children, is a hard-core worrywart. First: the chance of serious injury or death every time they get in a car is worrisome, too. Second: they will never be more alive than when they are staring this risk down and performing with their horse. All their senses, all their faculties, will be operating in the high range. It's just plain worth it. That doesn't mean I won't do plenty of worrying.

A good friend of mine with two boys of his own, both of whom have since grown up to be professional horsemen, once lamented the fact that in modern times it's just too easy for a boy to throw his leg over a motorcycle or ATV and too time-consuming and downright difficult for him to reach the same enjoyment level with a horse. He's right, and I'm proud that my kids are willing to make the extra effort. Their reward will be a world not of steel, glass, and asphalt but of animals, grass, and trees. And they will then become the ones who will work to preserve and protect that kind of world for their own children and for generations of children to come.

REMARKS AT DINNER FOR WINNING HUNT CUP JOCKEYS

When I won the Hunt Cup, and I was standing around afterward in my dazed euphoria, Duck Martin came up to me and said softly, "Welcome to a very small club."

Well, we *are* a very small club. We have shared experiences that no one else has, and nobody can take that away from us.

We've all sat in that awful little tent waiting for our horses to be brought to the paddock. Inside, "The quiet ones get loud and the loud ones get quiet." (I think those words were originally penned by Siegfried Sassoon about boys about to come out of the trenches into no-man's-land in World War I.)

We've all walked up to the sixth and sixteenth fences, and most of us have actually gotten a horse over—or more accurately our horse has gotten us over—them. As to you who have had the mixed fortune to find one or more rails down when you got there, I can only give you sympathy. It would be like saying you rode around Aintree, but they left out the Chair!

And all of us have had the happiest moment of our lives right there at the bottom of Snow Hill. All, that is, except for our Irish amateur jockey member. "Being Irish," Mark has, as William Butler Yeats put it, "an abiding sense of tragedy, which sustains him through temporary periods of joy!"

Finally, we've all, or most of us have, had to rear up on our hind legs in a room full of inebriated, scarlet-coated men, and women in bosom-baring gowns, and deliver . . . an . . . *oration.*

Now I didn't win my Hunt Cup till my fifth try. Before that, I had two seconds, a third, and a hard fall while upsides for the lead at the twentieth. The jockeys on either side of me at that moment, Russell Jones and Buzzy Hannum, are here in the room. A photographer snapped a photo of me on my hands and knees, staring at the ground in a bewildered stupor. What the photographer didn't catch was that a moment later a spectator leaped over the snow fence in front of the parking lot that became Cal Ripken's house and, without saying a word, pressed an ice-cold Heineken into my hand, restoring my faith in . . . something.

But anyway, what I was starting to say was that up till then I had prepared four different and perfectly usable, but subsequently unused, Hunt Cup winning jockey speeches. Back in those days, the sacred *duty* to give a speech that night at the Hunt Ball if you won was just as onerous as thoughts of the sixteenth fence . . . if you were on a good jumper, even more so.

Now the best winning rider speech I ever heard was given by Buzzy Hannum. That was back in the days when there was a notorious rivalry between the Green Spring Valley and Unionville as to who was more . . . skilled . . . at winning Hunt Cups. I think it might have been Frank Bonsal who originally threw down the gauntlet to our neighbors up north.

Well . . . Buzzy got up there and delivered about half an hour of unremediated . . . taunting . . . of the Valley boys. It was hilarious. The Maryland . . . tables . . . were absolutely *enraged!* Stokes Lott (whose credentials were that he rode in one Hunt Cup and fell at the second fence) got up and wanted to fight Buzzy . . . then and there. Poor Stokes, upon receiving his inheritance, became Baron von Pantz, moved to Key West, and died, but not before winning a couple of Ernest Hemingway lookalike contests. But that's a story for another time.

As to the *worst* Hunt Ball speech, it's a tie. On the one hand, we have my friend Johnny Bosley, who stood up in front of the crowded dining room and . . . free associated . . . for about an hour. He veered from topic to topic, none of them interesting, until finally, and I think this is the only time this happened at that particular venue, one began to hear shouts of "SIT THE F*&% DOWN!"

If my recollection is correct, Johnny was storming the podium at another Hunt Ball where he didn't win, doubtless with more reflections to unburden himself of, when he was intercepted by Security and escorted back to his table. But that's also a story for another time.

Tied for worst winning rider oration is Charlie Fenwick, Jr., affectionately known by his friends (behind his back) as *Junior*. Junior delivered many winning rider speeches, as you know, and they were all . . . relentlessly . . . *dull*. So monotonous that, now that I think of it, I might have heard some shouts from the audience then, too. So generally unentertaining that the organizers of the Hunt Ball decided that, what with Junior winning the Hunt Cup every year, they needed to put someone else up there on the Hunt Ball stage to galvanize the audience, for whom ticket prices were soaring and who needed *something* for their money (other than the bared bosoms across the table).

And thus was the Code of the Gentleman Jockey unraveled, and the practice of the Hunt Ball "Speaker" born. Now the Speaker introduces the winning horse's connections, including the jockey, and everybody is allowed to say something. So they all congratulate each other warmly, and then somebody tells the story of the horse.

Often this segment of the proceedings is about as long as Joe Davies's podcast, which was interesting enough, but at the Hunt Ball people need to remember the words of a wise racetracker: "*Every* horse has a story. Unless they win the Kentucky Derby, nobody wants to hear it!"

I was the Hunt Ball Speaker once or twice. Actually, they invited me to do it again this year, but I respectfully declined. Back in the day, I was about halfway through my Speaker's remarks when a member of the Hunt Ball Committee (they get to stand up there, too, now) *hissed* at me. *Hissed!* "Don't forget to thank Duck!" So I thanked Duck. I've often wondered, though, what exactly would happen if some year they *forgot to thank Duck.* Scary thought, but between you and me, *nothing will happen.* The Hunt Cup *will* be kicked off Snow Hill, and possibly sooner rather than later, but only if the National Steeplechase Association persists in sending Damon Sinclair to turf the hillside in front of Duck's house with his Chevy Suburban full of video equipment!

Back when I was practicing law, I was instrumental in Kathy Kusner becoming the first lady jockey allowed to ride in the Hunt Cup. (I haven't been invited to dinner in the Valley since.) But women have proved themselves more than up to the task, not only here at the Hunt Cup but elsewhere in steeplechasing, in the United States and internationally. I recently heard that French authorities either actually have, or are considering, giving lady riders a four-pound allowance, to promote the inclusion of more of them in the sport. There is a strong counterargument going on that this will eventually lead to them winning *everything*!

Whatever that may be, the inclusion of women among Hunt Cup riders has also contributed to the further unraveling of the Code of the Winning Rider. Now the winning lady rider can excuse herself from attending the Hunt Ball and giving a speech by simply saying, "I can't get a babysitter." End of discussion. At least the lady riders heretofore using that excuse have been married, but I'm sure the day of the *unwed* winning lady rider mother is coming. Alas.

Mikey Smithwick once said to me that the Hunt Ball was the worst party he ever had to attend. And this from the man who would have more different . . . society . . . women hanging off him that night than anyone in history. Crompton Smith would have been a close second in the numbers, but his bounty of beauties tended to call at the house where he lived the next day. I saw it all. Will never forget it.

I only bring this up because it's the *speech*, not the winning ride, that stirs up the women. So all you riders out there with thoughts of future glory better start thinking about what you're going to say!

It's a small club, just like Duck said. For a few years I'd say these words to the winning rider, too. I don't know if Duck kept on doing it. Maybe *every* successive winner does it now until the winning rider can scarcely make it back to the jockey's tent without twenty-five people whispering to him about small clubs. Actually, I hope they do. It's kinda cool.

TONG

I buried my friend in a wooded glade,
And on his body his halter I laid,
His name there in proud letters displayed,
I buried my friend in a wooded glade.

I cut a memento from his tail today,
A handsome wisp of black and bay,
And then I heaped the soil o'er
Midst images from days of yore.

I saw a colt at his mother's side.
He came to us not easy to ride.
Vivian trotting him over a rail,
His first races, memories so dim and pale.

Sometimes we won, sometimes we were too slow;
My God it seems a long time ago.
Then in 1980 the glory came,
The Virginia Gold Cup, and fame.

But that was nothing to what lay ahead,
Memories more distinct now in my head.
The first Hunt Cup a gift to me from his heart,
Then one for Liz, who rode him beautifully from the start.

We share our time here with just a few,
Fewer still enrich our lives by what they do.
Courage, dignity, and a generous soul
Defined Tong, I think, filling in this hole.

No one will ever know what he did for me,
But I will, I'll have that memory,
And that is something I shall always save.
I buried my friend in a wooded glade.

III

HUNTING

AND

FISHING

RUSSIA

June 16, 1997, 2 a.m., Arctic Circle,
Varzuga River, Kola Peninsula, Russia

The solstice was at hand. There would be no darkness. The sun had descended no lower than just below the tops of the tall fir trees that lined the bluffs overlooking the broad river. The light was dissipated, filmy. In it, the birch groves were luminescent, evoking the desperate energy of a brief annual time of growth. The rippleless surface of the river before us reflected the cloudless sky with a pale, intoxicating glow.

The fishing camp slept deeply. Nestled in the trees, it was bathed in a caliginous half light, and when we walked through on the way to the river, there had been no sound save gentle snoring through cabin walls.

We prepared to fish a point at the bottom of the island on which the camp stood. As we tied on flies, there was a familiar and unmistakable sound from far out in the river. The reverberating *thunk* of wood striking wood on the deck of a small boat. An ancient-looking, red-painted freight canoe passed in the distance with silent figures standing poling in the bow and stern. The sight was haunting. It seemed to transport us back to the days before 1917 when this river, with its enormous runs of Atlantic salmon, had been the private fishing preserve of the czars.

My friend cast his line far out on the smooth water. The fly swung with the current. Suddenly there was the lunging sidelong strike of a large salmon. My friend's rod arched and his reel screamed till the backing showed. He recovered the line, then the fish jumped high out of the water and ran again. There was another jump, the fish shaking its head furiously. Where the fish leaped and where the line ran seemed utterly disconnected. Slowly, though, the fish was brought to shore. The barbless hook was removed and the fish briefly revived in the current, then released to continue its way to the gravelly spawning grounds upriver.

Later, as we walked back through camp to our cabins, we heard low murmurings from the cook tent. Our cook, a New Zealand Russophile, was still awake, deep in conversation with the Russian dishwasher, seeking the secrets of this remote place. The sun continued its lateral passage below the tree line. The camp slept and now we joined it.

****

The Kola Peninsula is bounded on the west by Finland, on the north by Norway and the Barents Sea (a portion of the Arctic Ocean), and on the east and south by the White Sea. The Kola's first inhabitants were the ancient, nomadic Saami who hunted caribou, reindeer, elk, bear, and hare in its forests and fished its rivers during the ice-free months from late May to October. In the fifteenth and sixteenth centuries, settlers from the Novgorod Feudal Republic to the south established permanent villages in several locations (including the mouth of the Varzuga). Construction of a railway from Saint Petersburg to the Arctic coast, completed in 1916, led to the building of Murmansk, now the world's largest city north of the Arctic Circle, which is not to say a great deal. The waters of the North Atlantic Drift, an extension of the Gulf Stream, keep Murmansk ice-free year round, and this enabled the city to become a major fishing and fish-processing center, as well as giving it strategic importance. The Allied convoys into Murmansk during World War II were a lifeline of food and military equipment and supplies to the Soviets. The submarines and surface vessels of Russia's Northern Fleet, most nuclear powered, are based on the Kola now; in fact the world's largest concentration of nuclear weapons and reactors is located here. Not surprisingly, the rivers of this heavily militarized region have been off limits for the last half century (although it is said that the cosmonauts were allowed to fish the Rynda). The result?

Present-day salmon fishing that equals or exceeds anything you read about of days long past on the great North American rivers.

****

Just how good is the fishing? On the Varzuga, you fish with your guide from nine thirty in the morning till six in the evening. Most days you travel with him by boat to pools up- or downriver. But some of the best pools lie just off the camp island, and if you figure dinner takes two hours and you don't really need breakfast, that leaves thirteen and a half more hours for fishing them. The people who run the camp like you to catch lots of fish, and they keep a careful record of the totals, which are, as far as I could make out, always high. The reason for the diligent scorekeeping is that the value of a river, or more specifically the value of a week's fishing on the river, as well as the relative value of any specific week in the salmon run—a week in late May, for example, as opposed to a week in mid-June—is based on the previous catch history for that river and week. So if you combine management's desire for high totals with the fact that salmon angling can by its nature become very competitive, there's powerful reasons why people get sucked into what I call "the numbers vortex." The oft-ignored axiom is "Gentlemen don't count" (the number of fish they catch). As gentlemanly a gentleman as I ever knew, however, once entered his catch totals in the log book of another salmon camp and then added the words "It is not enough merely to succeed; others must FAIL!" One of our group on the Varzuga, an unassuming, reasonably companionable and very intelligent Irishman, got pulled into the numbers vortex to the tune, he told us jauntily, of an astounding 106 salmon landed in six days! There are salmon rivers with familiar names where people pay big money and might come away after a week with only a couple of fish landed. Or fewer.

****

Actually, I learned that this can happen on the Kola, too. Several weeks after our return I called a friend of mine, a veteran of many weeks angling for Kola salmon. I knew he had just returned from a week on a river. "How was it?" I asked. "Terrible," he said. "There were no fish in the river, and the agent put fifteen rods into a camp designed for twelve." My friend had been fishing a river with little history, and perhaps the outfitter had mistimed the run of salmon, as well as the number of bunks in camp. Indeed, variety is the name of the game in everything about the fishing experience to be had on the ten or so Kola rivers now open to foreign anglers. The main river leases are held by British (Varzuga, Pana, Kitza), American (Ponoi), and Swedish (Umba, Kharlovka, Litza, Rynda, Yokanga) interests. The salmon runs generally begin at ice-out in late May and continue into early July, with the larger fish coming into the rivers first, but the individual rivers vary in size and numbers of fish to be expected at any given time. Also, there is a documented autumn run of salmon in at least one river, the Ponoi, which is now being studied (and booked for fishing). The comforts of the various fishing camps themselves perhaps differ most of all. Food ranges from "frankly appalling" to gourmet, accommodations from more than comfortable to—in the recent case of my friend—nonexistent, travel between pools on the river from jet boat speed and comfort to scrambling along the rocks, and so forth. The Russian guides, I would guess, are pretty much alike from river to river.

****

Our guides were from the small village (three hundred people, twelve cars) of Varzuga. They're not your heralded Masters of the River in the great Scandinavian, North American, or European gillie tradition, although they might become so with time, but they're perfectly capable of peering into your fly box with you and showing you the one that might work, tying it on if need be, pointing out where on the river a fish might be found if you throw your line there, and then netting and releasing your fish fairly skillfully when the time arrives. Fairly skillfully. They tell a story of a guide the previous year, "Lyorsha the Lunger," who, when a fish was hooked, would grab the line and run down it like a cowboy calf roper, far into the river, bent on subduing the fish without further angler aid. Somehow the legendary Lyorsha is said to have actually gotten a nine-pound salmon, still on its first run and at least fifty yards into the backing, into his net!

Our guide for the week was Ivan (pronounced "Yvonne"), and it was his first year on the river. There was a Sergei and a Fyodor, too. Ivan was so glad to have this job for two and a half months of the year that I'd sometimes catch him sitting on the lumpy metal fuel tank of the boat while Allan, the British camp manager, ran us upriver, gazing up at Allan like nothing so much as a large, devoted spaniel.

The guides could all say, "Nice fish!" in perfect English, and "Excellent!" but not much more. Come to think of it, this might have been all they needed, since the largest part of their pay came directly from the anglers in the form of tips at the end of each week. But Ivan hungered for more English, as we learned the first day when, after grilling us a salmon on the riverbank for lunch, he reached into his fishing vest and pulled out an English-Russian dictionary and a kind of phrase translation book intended to help translate useful thoughts such as "My father works in an agricultural collective" and, no kidding, "California!" into English.

We had many stream-bank language sessions with Ivan over the course of the week. The teaching and learning ran both ways. Here's what we learned: The Russian words or phrases for "big," "little," "fish," "fisherman," and "fishing," all important notions on the river. Also the word for "hat," after a member of our party fell in all the way up to his while wading. The words for the civilities "please," "thank you," "hello," "good morning," "goodbye," and "cheers" (as to the latter, it is probably a bad idea to make the mistake I made of settling down after dinner one night to drink vodka by the shot with the Russians). And grown-up things to call people, like "whore!" and "head of cock!" and something unthinkable for a retort when somebody calls you "head of cock!" And the f-word. In Russian pronounced "zabish." We would practice on the other guides: *"Dobre utra*, Sergei" (good morning). *"Zabish."* Sergei: "Excellent!"

****

Russia's last hundred years or so of social hypertension and state brutality have implications for the angler from abroad, no matter how purely Izaak Waltonian the purposes of his visit. I must say, though, we were well prepared for this by our outfitter, who warned in no uncertain terms that it would be better to submit to what was coming, then enjoy the magnificent fishing that lay, sooner or later, ahead, than to resist or disrupt in any way and spend the rest of your life breaking rocks in Siberia. So when we initially arrived on the Finnair flight from Helsinki to Murmansk, we disembarked hopefully, took a picture or two outside the terminal before being herded inside and the door padlocked, then waited three and a half hours while . . . what? There was only one international flight a week to "process." There were scores of officials, in and out of uniform. There were even nice-looking lady officials in uniforms and military greatcoats with black military high heels on their tiny little feet that conjured up a "Girls of the Gulag" type of personal fantasy. But we all just sat there, those who could find seats. The one-room washroom was worse than filthy. There was nothing to eat or drink. The whole thing was nothing but an elbow in the ribs from the Bolshois, and eventually it ended. When we finally got to camp, the fishing was as advertised.

****

Early in the morning of the last day, the twin-turbine 3,000-horsepower Mi-8 rumbled over the trees and settled slowly to its landing pad, a wildflower-strewn meadow adjacent to camp. Two soldiers in camo with AKs got out. We threw in our gear, waved to our guides, and clambered inside, followed by the soldiers. I sincerely hoped the guns weren't loaded. The navigator smiled at us, replaced his plywood bench between the pilot's and copilot's seats, and sat down on it, his chart across his knees. Seat belts "weren't necessary," we had been told on the flight in, and there weren't any anyway. The great aircraft roared, shuddered, lifted, tilted forward, and started us homeward.

I looked down at the dark waters of the Varzuga and thought of another river:

> Ah, how should I, the gentle Don, not flow trou-
> bledly?
> From my depths, the depths of the Don, the cold
> springs beat;
> Amid me, the gentle Don, the white fish leap.
>
> —Old Cossack song from *And Quiet Flows
> the Don* by Mikhail Sholokhov

Author's note: The following poem has nothing to do with fishing, but I wrote it early one morning while waiting for breakfast at Boca Paila, the Mexican flats fishing camp where many of my friends and family fished with me for years and years. I'm including it here because in a small way it reminds me of the gorgeous Yucatan coast south of Tulum and the many happy days on the bays of Boca Paila.

THE BROWN DOG
AND THE LITTLE BOY

The rising sun shimmers on a calm sea,
Sends shafts of light through billowing clouds
And coats the palm leaves in gold.

But inside only half light;
A thin brown dog curled in a ball, nose to tail
Sleeping on a soft chair
And me with a cup of coffee.

A little boy with tousled hair, eyes full of sleep
Pushes through the door, crosses the room,
    vanishes somewhere.
The dog raises his head, then hops to the floor
And trots as if late to catch the boy.

Was there a plan? None that I could see,
Yet this sleepy boy and dog that didn't stir for me
Have passed by and out of this still darkened room
Like a general and his army.

And so it is with little boys and dogs
On shores gilded by rising suns everywhere.
A fundamental force binds the pair.

ROCKFISH

"This might not be such a good idea, hotshot," said the mariner's angel who sits on my shoulder and spews out advice in situations like this. The wind was gusting strongly, and I had the *Anna Banana* upwind of Pooles Island's rocky shore. I'd dinged the propeller before shutting off and raising the 200-horsepower Johnson motor. Then the anchor had shown no inclination to dig in on the gravelly bottom. Finally it set, for now, and I was hand-over-handing out line to get as close as I dared to the sudsy backs of the waves breaking on the shore.

Sounds dumb, I'll admit, but my companions and I were thinking instead about all the good reasons to be exactly where we were. Those waves building all the way from the Bay Bridge were full of baitfish, now tumbling and churning among the Pooles Island rocks. It was evening, and rockfish, huge rockfish, would have abandoned the depths and be prowling the shallows, hungry. It was nearly dark, so other boats, anchored off or trolling in the safety of deeper water, wouldn't see what we were up to or start a stampede if we hit pay dirt.

We did. "There he is," yelled one of my fishermen as his rod doubled over. I could see his line leading right into the frothy backwash. "I can't hold him!" he shouted as the line spun off his ten-pound-class reel.

We got him, though, and more. Fish so big we had to measure each one to be sure they weren't over the thirty-six-inch limit. Strong, fresh, fighting monsters of rockfish. People travel thousands of miles—heck, I travel thousands of miles myself—to remote places

you can't even talk to by *radio* if weather conditions aren't right, to
find fishing like this. We caught these fish twenty minutes from *Anna
Banana*'s dock.

How very lucky we Marylanders are. The rockfish is truly "our"
fish, for the Chesapeake is the spawning ground for 90 percent of the
East Coast's rockfish population. And this rockfish season, from the
long Atlantic swells of the Chesapeake Bay Bridge-Tunnel to the swirl-
ing foot of Conowingo Dam, from the black depths of the ship chan-
nels to tangled woody deadfalls far up the Bay's tributary rivers, the
rockfish were dispersed and "available" in sizes and numbers not seen
since the 1960s. (Speaking for myself, I think the adjective "available"
is abrasive when used like this. Artichokes are "available" at Safeway.
Christmas turkeys are "available" at the Hess store. A rockfish in his
native habitat is "available"? I don't think so. But that seems to be the
fishing writer vernacular.)

The rebounding rockfish population is an outstanding tribute
to nature's bounty, and her resilience, and man's restraint. As Tom
Horton wrote in his 1987 collection of lyrical essays, *Bay Country*:

> The rock may live several decades and attain nearly
> the length and weight of a man, and during all that
> time they choose to hug our coastal edges, feed in
> the shallows, and return each spring from the length
> of the East Coast to procreate in Chesapeake rivers
> almost to the doorsteps of our towns and cities—
> accessible to, and vulnerable to, us as are few other
> wild species of their stature. . . . How we treat them
> says a good deal about our progress in learning to co-
> exist with nature.

Well, pat ourselves on the back. Especially pat on the back the
biologists, fisheries managers, and most especially, the politicians
who acted in 1984 to impose a complete moratorium on rockfish
fishing so that the 1982 "class" of rockfish could mature to spawning age. Pat Mother Nature on the back for allowing the rockfish's
spawning year of 1989 to be a near complete success in spite of acid

rain, toxins, nutrients, sediments, and all the other ways we humans contaminate the watershed.

Now we're experiencing once again a truly great recreational fishery Bay-wide. What to do next? For one thing, we need to bite the bullet and finally end all commercial fishing and all commercial sales of rockfish caught in the wild. I make this suggestion with reluctance, because the proceeds from rockfish landings can be a very important supplement to a waterman's income. On the other hand, how can you and I be expected to respect the resource and practice a conservation ethic when rockfish are being hauled up by the ton right across the Bay? Further, it doesn't any longer make sense to thus dilute a globally important recreational fishery, attracting an extremely large number of people, with economic consequences for a vast number more. The sale of wild Atlantic salmon, venison, waterfowl, and other wild meats has long been prohibited, deemed necessary to save each such species from extinction. Several types of finfish, most particularly the rock, now require similar protection.

For the first part of this fall's rockfish season, Maryland anglers who requested them were issued two rockfish tags. These non-locking paper tags invited abuse. The DNR needs to have indestructible tags that are immediately and permanently locked to the fish when the fish is landed. The tags need to be linked to a specific tidal fishing license and, perhaps, an extra fee charged for them as with deer tags. The proceeds from rockfish tag sales could be dedicated to both enforcement of rockfish regulations and stocking of young fish.

If there were no commercial netting, the recreational rockfish season might be twice as long and be divided into segments, spring and fall, when the water is cool and the release of under- or oversized fish can more likely be accomplished safely. More on that later. Depending on the fish population, the DNR might then sell each sportsman five, six, or seven tags, to be used over the whole season. No special consideration for charter vessels. People could fill their tags on board like anywhere else.

These days, it can be hard *not* to catch rockfish when fishing for other species. Catching and releasing rockfish is currently subject to rules, or lack of them, which are confusing at best and at worst a severe problem. It is estimated that up to 90 percent of the rockfish caught and released from the Conowingo Dam catwalk during the warm summer months die from the ordeal. Similarly, studies show that during the same time of year, as many as a hundred out-of-season fish die daily after being released in the Chesapeake from Pooles Island northward. Many of these have been hooked using live eels. The fact is that anadromous fish like the rockfish and Atlantic salmon, which live most of their adult life in the ocean but return to their native freshwater rivers to spawn, are more and more vulnerable to stress mortality as water temperatures increase and salinity decreases. This explains the approach used on some of the warmer Canadian salmon rivers. If you land a legal fish you *must tag* and keep him, and then since the limit is one fish per day, you *must* retire from the river. They estimate that more fish are saved this way than if the angler stayed all day catching and releasing fish that would die later. Loving them to death, so to speak. We need to stop loving our rockfish to death like this.

Under certain circumstances, though, legalized catch-and-release fishing can offer a fairly optimal use of the resource and one not without—as this year's Bassmaster Classic (all catch and release for smallmouth and largemouth bass) showed—impressive economic consequences. During the three days of fishing, 423 fish were boated, brought to the Civic Center, filmed for delayed broadcast on the Nashville cable network, and then released back into the Bay. Five fish died. General Motors thought enough of the proceedings to unveil two of its 1992 models, cars that the local Chevy dealers hadn't even seen pictures of, at the accompanying Bassmaster Classic outdoors show.

Rockfish catch-and-release mortality appears not to differ too much from that of bass if you factor in cool water, high salinity, and artificial lures only, as opposed to natural baits such as live eels, which tend to be ingested deeply into the fish, making removal of the hook difficult and bloody. Maybe at the proper time of year and place we could have a rockfish catch-and-release season, too.

Whatever we do, our relationship with the rockfish will require constant reevaluation and tinkering. The important thing will be the demonstration that we humans, at the top of the food chain, have enough wisdom to keep the rockfish in the equation. For this reason

I turn again to Tom Horton. Better yet, read him yourself. From *Bay Country*:

> A man who lived and wrote decades ago on a scrub farm in the Sand Hills of Wisconsin, and, as far as I know, never caught a rockfish, came closest to explaining their allure. Aldo Leopold, the conservationist, understood there are values to living creatures that, although unquantifiable, are as universal as any of the laws of science; the physics of beauty he called it—one department of natural science still in the Dark Ages: "Everybody knows for example that the autumn landscape in the north woods is the land, plus a red maple, plus a ruffed grouse. In terms of conventional physics the grouse represents only a millionth of either the mass or energy of an acre. Yet subtract the grouse and the whole thing is dead."

AUTUMN IDYLL

Fear and Loathing in the Middle Bay

"Most likely they all died from it," Bill Goldsborough, fisheries biologist and soft-spoken giant of the rockfish recovery saga, told me later. "Their gill structure is too delicate to withstand the abrasion from being strung over the side of the boat on a rope like that." Those two men in their eighteen-foot skiff had thought they were mighty smart, though. They had everybody fooled, you damn betcha.

They'd catch a fish, hold him up, and look him over carefully, then either throw him back or glance about to see if anybody was watching and shift him to a stringer suspended off the bow. Then when they'd had enough fishing for the day, they'd keep the two biggest and cut the rest loose. The rules outlaw this "culling," as it is called, but the rules didn't seem to be in force here. Five years of rockfish moratorium and four more years of conservative fishery management so these jerks could jack around with the law to take home a fatter fish! Swine. But, hey, they would go to fishermen's heaven compared to another group we heard about on another day from our captain, Bobby Marshall, a young man with a family to feed whose livelihood partly depends on taking people sport fishing for rockfish, something he is very good at.

Bobby watched this other party of jackals catch their limit, which for private boats is one fish per man per day, and put them in the cooler. After this, they kept on fishing, which is perfectly legal as long as it's catch and release, until they landed a huge fish. As quick as you please, out of the cooler came a smaller, dead rockfish, which they flipped into the water. Into the cooler went the new trophy. Bobby yelled across the water at them. They gave him the finger. Then they started putting every fish they caught into the cooler. That'll teach that meddler a lesson. Bobby called the game wardens, but they never showed up.

The group of friends and fishermen I was with, who had chartered Bobby for the day, had spent the night at Saint Michaels, a weird and dysfunctional little sinkhole enjoyed mainly by Washington politicians and their secretaries. In the pre-dawn blackness of the following day, we motored the twenty or so miles out to Tilghman Island to meet Bobby at his boat. Tilghman is still for the most part an authentic and exciting place, reverberating with the sound of workboat engines and driven by the rhythms of tide and season.

Unfortunately, there is also a new yacht club residential development with a phony English-sounding name, an old hotel-restaurant-sportfishing center where we got rude treatment at breakfast, and an alternative-lifestyle marina where they are often seen in warm weather posturing at the end of the gas dock. But it was cold now as we passed by the place in Bobby's forty-foot Tilghman-built workboat and headed for Stone Rock, a well-known and reliable fishing spot twenty minutes south.

Soon we lay easily at anchor. Bobby had us positioned in what appeared to be the prime location in a fleet of twelve or fifteen boats, mostly charters. At least we were the ones doing the most leaning over the transom, either to release undersized rock or to net and bring aboard those that were clearly keepers. The scene seemed right: rockfish season, fish heavily schooled up, men making an honorable living on the water while their "sports" enjoyed the unmatched leisure of recreational angling. Then a boat appeared in the distance on our port bow, growing rapidly larger. We heard the beginnings of an engine roar as the craft bore down on us. Somehow, Bobby Marshall knew what was about to happen and leaped to the bow of his boat. As the intruder, a new and expensive Slickcraft Tiara 3500 Express, passed deafeningly at full throttle not thirty feet from us, splitting the anchored fleet, throwing up a huge wake, and sending all the rockfish somewhere else, Bobby heaved a solid lead ten-ounce pyramid sinker directly at her windshield.

"Damn!" he exclaimed, as the projectile fell harmlessly in the wake of the rogue vessel. "Didn't lead him enough!" If Bobby'd caught the malignant Anglerphobe directly between the eyes, fifty eyewitnesses would have sworn it never happened.

Fishing over and time on my hands, I detoured home through downtown Easton, past the Tidewater Inn and Bullitt House, new wealth run amuck, the old gentlemen who somehow added a note of grace and humor to the whole tawdry business all dead now, replaced by people in Grand Cherokees.

Then across Route 50, here a hell-blight of fast food, gas station, and motel pit stops for people who live somewhere else. Finally out past the twin landfill mountains, the police firing range, and the sewerage plant effluent evaporation fields, past the almost unknown wild cherry grove wherein stands the "batwing" tombstone of Rebecca Harrison, who died at age thirteen in 1739 from the plague. Buried alongside is her brother Samuel, who died at age five, the last vestiges of an ancient and all but forgotten settlement. Then on down the grown-over two-track lane to my duck "club" on the Choptank River, one of the great places anywhere until a local lawyer ruined it by building his garish mansion right across the river and square in the middle of one thousand pristine acres of tide-charged, duck-feeding, rockfish-spawning, and mosquito heaven.

Inside my shack, enormous snake skins are hanging from rafters, in fragments on the floor, and curled over the banister of the stairway to the sleeping loft. The place needs to be burned down, the energy that kept it decent, and the snakes out, now gone. Not even an empty bottle of Mount Gay to remind of past post-hunt mortems. I fish and hunt in other, wilder places now, when I can. The Native Americans had the same reaction when the Colonial settlements began. Look what good it did them.

McCREADY HOSPITAL

Horse Hammock Point on Smith Island was once a place of lush cattle pastures, wooded groves, orchards, and vegetable plots. All of that is now completely beneath the waves, save for a small piece of marsh not much bigger than our eighteen-foot skiff. As we approached, lean and dark things stood up from the grass there. They turned out to be twenty or so cormorants, which rose and departed in single file as we idled closer. The surrounding water was dappled with shadows, an ancient stump field.

The angler in the bow made a smooth backcast, then sent his weighted green Clouser minnow fly ahead. One quick retrieving strip of the line . . . two . . . and the rod doubled over violently. In the shallow water a sudden glimpse of long silver flank. Boat side, a beauty of twenty-two inches or more. We couldn't legally invite the rockfish aboard, though, so we gently released him. The rockfish season here in Virginia wouldn't open for several more weeks.

Earlier that day, slack low tide at our Maryland fishing spot three quarters of a mile to the north had sent us into these waters to pass the time; the incoming tide would run sooner here. Now it was time to head north again, across the state line.

We were men on a mission. It was opening day of the fall rock season in Maryland, and I had promised the family a rockfish dinner Sunday night. The assistant fish chef already had been dispatched to the grocery store for the other necessary ingredients. The cooler in my truck back at the ramp held enough blocks to ice down a caribou.

When we arrived back in Maryland waters, at the western approach to Smith Island's Big Thorofare, the incoming tide was gurgling by the black jetty boulders. Perfect. But another boat was anchored there, blocking access to our prime fishing spot. Three sad-looking fishermen sat aboard, slinging things that looked like bluefish trolling baits in the direction of, but not quite close enough to, the jetty rocks. We scowled at them and motored around to the less productive water on the other side of the jetty, where we dropped a stern anchor.

Then the three of us all cast our Clouser minnows at once. In a short time, our "friends" in the other boat were observing our multiple hookup, and in due course our onboard cooler held a limit of legal-sized rock. The other guys began frantically scouring their tackle boxes for anything that looked like a green Clouser minnow.

It was no mean feat that we three men could all cast at once in a boat this small. Besides, as metal zinged here and there, everybody was a little jumpy after what had happened the last time we'd gone out together.

We had been fishing Great Point, an excellent spot quite close to Crisfield. I was slumming with lures, not flies. Suddenly, the rattletrap lure I was using snagged on something just under the surface of the water, possibly a stump. I pulled hard and straight back to try to dislodge it, a mistake, because the next thing I knew something hit me on one of my temples with tremendous force. Half-stunned, I waited for it to drop in my lap. It didn't. I reached up and jiggled the lure gently to see if it would fall out, the way lures usually do. Something warm and wet trickled through my fingers.

While this was taking place on my boat, one of my friends was casting to submerged stumps from a nearby point on the shore, while the other was in the process of landing a fish farther down the bank. I called the first. "Uh, could you come over and take a look at something here?" I could tell by the look on his face when he arrived and peered at my head that I had a problem. When my other friend arrived, he peered in turn and looked even gloomier.

Crisfield has the only hospital accessible to boats on the Bay—the Edward McCready Memorial Hospital—and soon we were landing at its dock. There was a nurse outside the emergency room door, smoking a cigarette.

"Can you walk?" she said as I walked up the pier.

"Yes," I said.

"Well, walk through to Admitting and come back here when you have the paperwork," she said.

I wandered through the hospital corridors in a mild state of shock. I stopped at a mirror. My friends had cut away the lure so that just one treble hook stuck out of my temple, along with some blood. It looked terrible.

I waited a very long time while the Admitting person (not Miss Hard Crab Derby, by any means) went through the paperwork with a sailor with a jammed knuckle. Finally, my turn came.

"Problem?" Admitting asked without looking up.

"I've got this fish hook stuck in my head," I said.

"OH MY GOD, DON'T MAKE ME LOOK AT IT," she gasped, averting her gaze even more.

A matronly nurse appeared to do Admitting's looking for her. "I wish they wouldn't send them up here to Admitting first," she pronounced.

"Me, too," I agreed.

Eyes downcast, we somehow got through the paperwork. Then I went back to the emergency room, where they had a doctor with a lot of experience in fish hooks. He did a great job, but it took a long time. If the thing had hit my eye, I'd be blind.

I never again cast a line without wearing glasses, and I make everybody on my boat do the same.

WILLY WARNER,
1980–1991

It was New Year's Eve morning. With the utmost gentleness, Dr. Steve Wilson confirmed to Liz and me our fear that the greatest favor we could do our old friend would be to have him put to sleep. The day before, Willy had been unable to avoid falling to the bottom of a steep bank near our back door. Later that same day, Brewster, a younger male who loved Willy and had never pretended to dominate, fought him savagely. This morning, I had found Willy lying away from the other dogs in a corner of the room where our dogs would never lie because it had been fouled by terrier "accidents." He was unable to rise. Always a very dignified dog, he wagged his tail feebly, as if to apologize for this embarrassment.

Willy was eleven years old, not ancient by any means, but his body was worn out, and now there was rapid and severe deterioration within his spinal column. Steve is a duck hunter. He had been in the marsh with Willy. No doctor, no funeral director, could have eased a family's sorrow better. Still, it was a very bad day.

A lifelong friend gave us Willy, a purple-pedigreed pup from Chesapeake City, as a wedding present. I named him Willy Warner after William W. Warner, the Pulitzer Prize–winning Chesapeake Bay naturalist and writer. Once, after a wonderful day's duck hunting, I sent my host a smoked salmon and signed the card "Willy Warner."

The host called the real Willy Warner and thanked the confused man effusively. Thus the two Willys knew of one another.

I had never owned or trained a gun dog before Willy. A lady in our community, Carolyn Ensor, whose knowledge of dogs and their training is boundless, helped me get started. She furnished me with two good books and some wonderful advice: keep your training sessions short, hold them regularly, and make sure your pupil is enjoying his work. I never used electrical collars or any type of electronic training device; I did use a dummy throwing gun a great deal. The first time I ever fired it, Willy ran two hundred yards the opposite way and hopped in my car! Take heart, ye who feel your charges are hopeless!

Willy was quickly to become the greatest retriever that I or anyone who ever hunted with me had ever seen. He had all the tools: He watched the birds keenly, he listened for that direction-giving thump or splash, he had a wonderful nose, he learned my hand and whistle signals, and he was willing to use them for guidance. He was tenacious. Once my brother and I watched him follow a swimming goose right over the horizon. Willy was hull down! My brother never got over that.

Some dogs love the thrill of the chase; some love the feel of still-quivering flesh in their mouth. Both such types have their dark sides, as you can imagine. What Willy loved most, however, was completing his job, delivering our quarry to my hand. He often gave out a sigh of rapture on doing so. He was all business. "Don't pat me, don't feed me, don't worry about how cold I am. Just knock down another one."

Knock 'em down and fetch 'em up we did! Bombay Hook, Miles River, Tred Avon, Choptank, Little Choptank, Deal Island, South

Marsh, Tangier, Assateague, Worton Point, Easton, Smyrna, Leipsic, Chestertown, my place, Tom's, Clinton's, Laddie's, Bobby's, Skip's. It was nothing to drive three hours, hunt three hours, and drive back three hours, all in one afternoon, and think it well worth it. Every retrieve was a work of art for me to watch and enjoy, a story unfolding with new and different nuances. Many were the times, with Willy and me alone together on a remote and windswept marsh, that I muttered to myself, "No one would ever, ever believe what I just saw!"

Willy accepted the working conditions as part of the job. He was scraped by ice, exhausted by relentless tidal currents, poked and scraped by dry marsh reeds. Once in Tangier Sound in January, he leaped from a boat into the salty water grown rubbery on the surface as it formed into ice. As he felt the searing cold, he let out a yelp and his eyes bulged out. He got the duck.

Too much percussion on the eardrums from gunfire eventually deafened us both, although Dr. Lumpkin was subsequently able to fix me. It was the beginning of the end for Willy, though. We hunted off and on a couple of years more, but, deprived of this essential sense, he couldn't do the job the way he was used to doing it, and this seemed to make him miserable. Also, his body was starting to ache and stiffen. For a couple of years, I didn't hunt at all out of consideration for his feelings. Then I started sneaking out of the house with Brewster, whom I'd half-trained surreptitiously. Finally Brewster and I would just load the gear and walk right by Willy, who'd never even raise his head. He knew, though.

There is a grove of trees to the west of our house where Willy and I spent countless hours with the dummy gun, a few minutes at a time, perfecting the tricks of his trade. There, where he used to bound off so joyfully in fulfillment of my commands, is where I buried him. I planted the year's live Christmas tree next to him. Steve had provided a nice shroud and cardboard coffin for Willy, and as the dirt covered it, I grieved. Do we grieve for the departed, or for ourselves? For loves lost, pages turned, chapters ended. In marsh, boat, and field, Willy and I were partners on this planet for a significant span of years, and now only one of us remained, lonely. Willy, for his part, had earned the immortality that all of us crave. For anyone who ever hunted with him, his memory will never die.

CORNUCOPIA

September, a Harford County Cornfield

The breeze is still hot, but the withered rustlings of still-standing corn whisper of seasonal change. In the distance, a silage chopper howls. A diesel school bus starts back up with a rumble after discharging a passenger. The sounds are reminders of time's passage, of endings and beginnings, somehow melancholy. Enough of that! Summer work at my own farm is now mostly finished, so there's no gloom for me as I stand at the edge of the cornfield. The dove hunt is about to begin.

A shot rings out. Another. Two more. At the far end of the field a retriever bounds straight as an arrow across the bare earth of newly cut corn. "Over your head," someone yells. I raise my gun, follow, lead, and fire without thinking. The bird hurtles groundward, his tiny cockpit engulfed in flames. No wonder this type of shotgunning was the number-one method of training our antiaircraft gunners before the advent of modern guidance systems.

Another shot. My bird falls at least thirty rows back in the standing corn. My Labrador, Brewster, comes back with the dove, his whole body wagging stiffly with pride. It would be hard to overstate the pleasure that hunting with a nice dog like this brings.

More shots. Misses, hits, retrieves. Even though I've been working Brewster in the weeks before the season begins to get him fit, and even though I've brought water with us out into the field for him to drink, still, in the heat and dust of the late afternoon, first his nose gives out and then his mind short-circuits completely. He lies propped against my leg panting heavily and loudly, sharing his discomfort with me most successfully. I'm still short of my twelve-dove limit, but that's OK. I'll thank the host and head home now.

Later these birds will be breasted and the breasts sautéed in bacon drippings with onions and mushrooms, simmered for an hour in a stock of celery soup with extra seasonings, and served with wild rice and a nice bottle of red Burgundy, something worthy, say a Louis Jadot Clos Vougeot 1987.

The best time of the year has begun.

October, Upper Chesapeake Bay, Near Pooles Island

To the west and north of my twenty-two-foot fishing vessel, *Anna Banana*, lie a hundred miles of bay, river, and creek shoreline preserved in its natural state, mostly unchanged since Captain John Smith sailed into these waters in 1608 and named the two-hundred-acre island aft of my vessel Powell's Island after one of his lieutenants. The island's name has been transformed into Pooles Island over the centuries that followed, but, thanks to the US Army, which purchased the whole area in 1917 to form Aberdeen Proving Ground and Edgewood Arsenal, the view from the water is pretty much what the explorers saw.

We aboard the *Anna Banana* are by no means alone on the water, for it is rockfish season. Things are going slowly at the moment for us, as well as for other boats in the vicinity. Then I get a call on the VHF. "*Anna Banana*, we're having a little luck over here." "Where?" I exclaim, followed by "DON'T ANSWER THAT!" as I envision heads swiveling toward radios in every boat that overheard the transmission. I ease away and find my friend. There are no other boats around. Not long after, one of my anglers shows me a line sizzling off the spool of her reel. "Hit him!" I shout, unnecessarily, for this lady knows a lot more about rockfishing than I do, and now her rod is acutely bowed as she throws her back into the fish. Minutes later, a stripe-sided, thirty-four-inch beauty is visible through the clear gray-blue water, the clearest water I have seen during my years on the Bay. We net the fish and dispatch him with a clean blow.

Gary Snyder is a distinguished natural historian-philosopher about whom another member of the same field once wrote, "I am somewhat discouraged by the thought that [he] has already said everything that needs to be said." Gary Snyder stresses in his works the wholeness of a natural world in which man's place is in balance with wild nature: "When an ecosystem is fully functioning, all the members are present at the assembly," he notes. Now, in the case of the Chesapeake Bay rockfish, civilized man, using intellect and will, employed the moratorium to restore such a balance. Maybe that is part of the reason why this fish, the first of three for our boat, all improbably large and beautiful, all legally caught and kept, makes us feel especially good.

When I get home, the rockfish will be filleted and the fillets sliced into medium-sized chunks. These will be dipped into a milk and egg batter, then coated with cracker meal that has been seasoned with Old Bay. Finally they will be cooked till golden brown in boiling peanut oil. The taste will be out of this world, and I will honor it with a bottle of something special, maybe a Corton-Charlemagne Domaine Bonneau du Martray 1988.

November, a Marsh on Shanty Gut,
Near Duck Creek, Delaware, 5:45 a.m.

We had hoped for wind, rain, fog, anything that might make waterfowl take to the air and not fly too high, but the stars had been glittering overhead as we walked from the lodge to the dock almost an hour ago. Now, decoys set, the boat hidden in a nearby tidal ditch, we wait for the sky to our east to begin the dawn neon light show that will herald a cloudless day.

Around us the cordgrass rustles softly in the light breeze, nearby ditches gurgle with the draining tide, and the rich smell of rotting detritus, the all-important primary link in the food chain, permeates everything. Why is a salt marsh so seductive? A friend once told me he thought it resonates something inside of us tracing all the way back to that day when our most distant ancestors first slithered up onto land to stay. Seems plausible enough to me. You want to visit in the right season, though. In September, when we repaired and brushed up our blinds, the mosquitoes and greenhead flies had been just marginally bearable. Once when I stopped at the lodge in June to pick something up on the way to the beach, they literally drove me, running, back into my car in two or three minutes. A man or dog would have gone mad after an hour of such torment.

Wingbeats low and fast over the blind. Not a flapping, more a rush of air, like a passing jet. Teal, I guess. Headed down the creek. *Spluuuuuush.* I look out at the decoys. Dark ripples on the water tell me a live duck is now swimming in my rig, but it's still too dark to make him out. Another flock of about ten is momentarily silhouetted against the paling sky, bending their flight path for a high-speed look at my decoys before continuing on. Kaboom! Kaboom! Kaboom! Someone in the distance shoots before legal light. My duck leaves, his wings beating the water as his ducky mind finally puts two and two together.

A couple of hours later we have the sunny, warm day we didn't want. We're telling stories, not watching the sky, parkas off, guns propped in the corners of the blind, glad to be where we are but not very optimistic, game-wise. Suddenly there are geese honking low behind the blind. A small flock returning from their inland cornfields to their Bombay Hook refuge, bereft, for whatever reason, of the counsel of a wise elder, who would have plotted a course far out of the range of any guns. My partner blows deep, expert, throaty notes into his call. "They're coming, still coming. NOW!" *BAM! BAM! BAM!* Splash . . . splash. A yelp of joy from Brewster, then . . . *splash!* as he hurls himself off the marsh bank in the direction of the two Canadas now lying motionless on the water.

Goose is a favorite in our house, and my wife does it like this: Breast the birds and then slice each breast latitudinally. Carefully cut the gristle out of the large, thin pieces. Pound them a while with a metal meat tenderizer. Dip in an egg and milk batter, then in bread crumbs, and fry in hot oil. The taste is tender, crisp, and light, yet rich and gamey enough. Or you can parmesan the thin, tenderized breasts. Either way, I think this deserves something dazzling. Champagne? Bollinger 1982!

TRACKS IN THE SAND

"This is a great spot. You go first," said Dan.

Wayne nodded and walked out to where the flat slab of bedrock sloped into the dark water. Dan sat down on a boulder and watched him strip off line and cast. Wayne's presentation was perfect. The fly settled to the surface and swung in an enticing arc. Nothing.

He stripped a little more line off the reel and cast again. Again nothing. With precision he covered the water of the pool. As he neared the pool's tail, an almost imperceptible droop slowly settled over his shoulders. That was Wayne, thought Dan. Good friend. Favorite fishing buddy. But either ebullient or despondent—nothing in between.

"No fish here," said Wayne, reeling in.

"Watch this," Dan said. Edging past Wayne, he walked out to the water's edge on the narrow rock slab, then waded in along it till the deepening current pushed alarmingly against his waders. The clear water on either side of the ledge looked bottomless and menacing. The roar from the mile of rapids and falls just upriver shut out all the world save the water before him. He stripped line and cast, stripped more line, and cast again. He let the fly swing at about the limit of Wayne's casts, then stripped more line and, double hauling, cast again, feeling in wrist and forearm the perfect and powerful flex of his fine 10-weight. The fly landed and made a little "V" on the smooth current as it began its swing. Suddenly there was a large swirl, almost frightening in its violence. He had a glimpse of a large Atlantic salmon's iron-red open jaws. Missed! He grinned over his shoulder at Wayne, whose mouth hung open with surprise. Dan made his way back to where Wayne stood. Wayne's body was no longer drooping. "Go back out there and catch him," Dan said.

Dan had been fishing this same week on the river for several years, but it was Wayne's first trip. At week's end, though, Wayne was top rod, no small accomplishment in a camp where most of the anglers knew the river well and fished hard. While himself fishing, Dan would occasionally glimpse his friend's lanky cowboy's body in the distance, clambering over rocks to prospect new pools; the vignette would usually end with the distant figure bending over and releasing something bright and silvery back into the water. At the camp party the last night, the two friends drank the last of the rum straight from Dan's flask and toasted the river, the salmon, and their own good fortune at having been there. "And to next year," said Wayne, "and the year after and the year after."

It was not to be. A year later, Dan stood on the same rock ledge and emptied the cellophane bag holding Wayne's ashes into the current. The tumor had done its work on Wayne swiftly, though certainly not kindly. His young widow had thought Wayne would be happiest here. "Weave, weaver of the wind." The great Irish novelist's words fit. A spasm of self-pity came, but Dan had expected it, and it passed. The granular bits were drawn into a back eddy and sank from view. He stood a moment longer, but the roar of the falls blunted his thoughts. He picked up his fly rod and started upriver.

****

September 1795

An enormous boulder stood in the center of the natural clearing. Next to it grew a lone spruce with lower branches broken off. Ajut was just able, jamming his body between the tree and the boulder's steep, lichen-covered side, to inch upward and closer to the spruce's first ring of downturned branches. Needles scratched at his face and broke off, some falling inside the collar of his caribou-hide summer parka. He grabbed a branch, which cracked but held, and pulled himself to a standing position in the fork of the tree, ten feet above the ground. From there he was just able, with a mighty effort, to leap across the gap between the tree and boulder to a precarious landing on the boulder's rough shoulder. Two steps along it brought him to his intended perch overlooking the clearing. He shook the spruce needles out of the bottom of his parka, adjusted the large flat river rock that someone had managed, years before, to haul up for a smooth seat, and settled down to wait.

They were due. As surely as the mighty river flowed north, the great stream of the caribou migration must now flow south as it always had when the scrub willow and speckled alder on the riverbank turned a golden yellow and the frost quelled the black flies for another year. Then the caribou, fat from their summer on the tundra plains, would head southward across the tree line toward the winter protection of the deep forests.

There are centuries-old caribou trails worn everywhere into the mossy floor of the forests, which stretch outward from the great river. But at the place where Ajut crouched atop his boulder, the animals' hooves had worn almost every bit of the ground vegetation away to bare sand and rock. At this spot along the river, the steep bedrock shoulders of a high inland ridge with an impassable tundra bog at its base constricted the flow of the herd so that all must pass through a narrow area no more than forty yards or so in width. For as long as anyone could remember, the Inuit hunters had come here by boat in early autumn to obtain the meat, tallow, and hides that would enable their people to survive the winter ahead.

Ajut knew the migration would come soon. There had been fresh wolf tracks on the sands of the killing plain each of the last three mornings when the hunters had come up from their camp at river's edge, and last night the wolves' howling had been almost continuous. A raven circled lazily on an airstream high above Ajut on his boulder. Wolf, raven, and man waited—predators whose winter survival would be wholly dependent on a common prey.

They were here! Ajut heard the cracking of scrub boughs and loud rustling and scraping as the incongruously large antlers of both bulls and cows penetrated the dense spruces. Fifty animals emerged from the trees at once, another hundred behind them, endless hundreds, Ajut knew, behind these. Ajut gave a low whistle and saw his friend Nanituk shrink silently into the shadow of a lone spruce. On all sides below Ajut, hunters now crouched in readiness behind boulders and trees, their spears held tensely as the animals approached.

The first rank of caribou was allowed to pass, oblivious to the motionless men, their eyes blank with the instinctive necessity of their movement to the south. Ajut saw that their hides were sleek and underlain with fat. He marveled, as he never failed to do, at the long, awkward, and disjointed-looking legs, which somehow carried the great animals with perfect ease and efficiency through bog and forest and over boulder field, gravel bank, and when necessary, across the mighty river itself. He noted the large, healthy crop of calves, some butting their heads against their unpausing mothers' udders in an attempt to nurse on the run, bumped forward by the wave of animals behind them.

Now Ajut gave a second whistle and, standing, plunged his long-handled spear deeply between the shoulders of a caribou that was pressed tightly against the boulder below him by the rest of the herd. At Ajut's signal, each man arrayed in hiding sprang to drive his spear into the nearest caribou. No animal could avoid the mortal stroke, as each was tightly crowded against its neighbor in a river of moving flesh. Nonetheless, each time a spear was driven home, the reaction was immediate and violent as the great animals reared upward, sometimes sprawling across the backs of the animals next to them, flinging their heads and great racks of antlers wildly from side to side. Bulls turned, dying, to charge their attackers, antler shovels forward, heads down, mouths frothing with blood. The men struck again and again till none had a spear, torn from their grasps or broken in the frenzied, dusty, bloody melee.

Then it was over. The main herd had diverted into the thick scrub between plain and river, some into the river itself to avoid the danger. Ajut stared about him at the aftermath, then, again using the lone young spruce for a ladder, made his way to the ground. Mortally wounded caribou filled the clearing. Some lay on their sides, legs thrashing. Others were still standing, barely, with legs splayed and heads held low, dripping blood. The hunters moved among them, deftly cutting the throat of each.

Ajut heard a man's dreadful scream and ran toward the sound. Coming around a large boulder, he saw that a huge bull had Nanituk pinned against the rock. The shovel on the front of the animal's mighty rack pierced Nanituk's groin. Blood frothed from the bull's mouth and nose as it lashed its head from side to side in a death rage, scraping Nanituk's body against the rough rock and lichen surface until the clothes were torn away. Ajut yelled and ran at the bull, which moved back, releasing Nanituk to slump to the ground. Another hunter ran up and stabbed at the animal with his spear as Ajut half dragged his friend around the boulder. Nanituk was able to struggle to his feet, then fell back in a sitting position against the rock. "It's not so bad now," he said. "It was . . . a good hunt." His eyes fell slowly until he gazed at the ground right in front of him. With a spasm of effort, he looked up again. "Ajut . . ." Nanituk said no more. Ajut saw that the sandy ground was dark with the lifeblood that had pulsed out from the severed artery high on Nanituk's leg.

***

September 1997—I

Where the river broadens above the constriction of Ten Mile Falls, they beached the outboard-powered freight canoe in the lee of a rocky point. Dan followed the old explorer up through the dense riverbank growth of scrub willows, leaves beginning to show blaze orange with the first frosts. They reached the plateau that marked the centuries-old level of extreme high water and penetrated the virgin black spruce forest.

There was no evidence of a path, but the old explorer seemed to know where he was going. Branches scratched Dan's face and tugged at his clothes. Then just ahead in the primordial setting loomed something clearly manmade—a great cairn of spruce trunks. Ancient-looking, its base itself spiked with spruce sapling and alder, its upper levels moss-covered and heavily weathered, the cairn had been constructed of mature trees, branches stripped away, laid against one another to form a solid tepee-shaped structure rising from the forest floor.

Here, thought Dan, rested the remains of someone whose way of life must have been that of the Stone Age. Eons of time were compressed dizzyingly in the edifice before him. A part of him wanted to try to dismantle it and discover the secrets hidden in its base. Yet, a stronger impulse was to disturb nothing. For whoever built this timber cairn atop the permafrost, life had been a day-to-day struggle. Still, there had been time enough to pause to honor and protect the body of a fallen comrade. Dan would not be the one to dishonor the action. He moved on through the forest behind the explorer.

They came to a large clearing. Here the ground, except for scattered boulders and a few lone spruces, was sandy. The usual soft, mossy ground cushion was largely absent. Had centuries' worth of migrating caribou hooves caused what amounted to a geomorphic change in the topography? Or was this an ancient beach on the river that was now three-quarters of a mile distant? As he puzzled over this, Dan came upon something that puzzled him even more. Before him on the brown sand lay a large oval of fifty or so small rocks, many with jagged fracture marks that indicated they came from a fast-moving part of the river. Some human hand had to have brought them here and arranged them in this way. Why? Dan imagined that this might have been the site of some kind of ceremony, possibly associated with a successful hunt. Again he felt wonder and a twinge of momentary intimacy with people of so long ago.

Now Dan saw a boulder, much larger than the others, near the center of the clearing, and he walked to it. Tall and steep-sided, it commanded the area. A lone spruce, scraggly with age, abutted the boulder, its lower branches missing. Dan saw that its middle branches were bent downward, as if by some repeated force at the point where they joined the tree's trunk. Wedging himself between rock and tree, he pulled himself up, using the downturned branches until he was able to reach the fork. Looking across at the top of the boulder, he saw that someone had placed a smooth, flat river rock on the rough lichenous surface, as if for a seat. Dan felt a chill and clambered down the old spruce to the ground.

On the far edge of the clearing, at a spot where moss still grew thickly, the old explorer pointed to something on the ground. Large tracks, toe of one at the heel of the next, were worn into and through the thick moss to the sand below. The explorer explained how a bear might follow the same circular thirty-mile route for his lifetime, leaving his memorial thus etched virtually permanently on the tundra.

Walking back across the clearing on their way back to the boat, they came across fresh wolf tracks, hundreds of them. "The caribou are getting nearer," the old explorer said.

****

September 1997—II

Back at the main fishing camp, Dan walked along the walkway of spruce-slab planking linking the row of cabins and tents with the main lodge. A shallow, polished furrow of wear ran down the middle of the walkway. So many good men had traveled this path over the years. Filled with anticipation as they pulled on waders and strung fly line through rod guides on that first afternoon in camp. Drinks in hand as they clumped in to dinner. Walking sleepy-eyed in the cool sunrise to breakfast. Rods held upright each morning for the wadered walk down to the canoes. Back in the evening with stories to exchange. Barefoot, carefully, to the shower tent. Maybe a little drunk at bedtime after the camaraderie of the dinner table. Looking up at midnight to see wondrous fountains of northern lights in a great arc across the whole ceiling of the sky. "Anybody else happen to see the aurora last night?" one angler had asked that morning at breakfast. "Yup!" chorused seven other fifty-pluses. Men with tender prostates. Dan had stepped outside last night, too. Now he chuckled in spite of himself.

So many now dead. "You'll know it's my last year when I stay for two weeks," old Jack had once said. He did and it was. Wayne, Dr. Bob, the old trial lawyer Ben. Gentlemen and fishermen. None ever knew for sure, when they walked down to the boats that last day for the short ride out to the waiting seaplane, whether they'd ever see the place again. Looking back over their shoulders at the island, a sentinel in the river. With its lonely flagpole, brave in the emptiness of the Arctic. Their own mortality the one question that couldn't be answered. The worn planking of the walkway to evoke their memory if they didn't make it.

****

September 1997—III

On the last day they had breakfast and packed up rods and gear. There would be a couple of hours until it was time to take the boats down-river to where the Otter landed. Dan took the path down to the rocky beach and walked along the shoreline. The island on which the camp stood, several acres in size, had a characteristic esker shape with dirt and boulders piled highest on the upriver side by the immense forces of spring ice-out and high water. Dan climbed to the highest point. Looking farther upriver, he could see where the broad valley of the river narrowed to the long section of falls and deep pools that held salmon so well. A caribou cow and calf picked their way across a gravel bar in the middle distance. The roar of distant falls filled Dan's ears. The timelessness of the place became a physical pressing on his chest.

He bent down to pick up a large, rounded rock and, struggling with its weight, set it against another. He would build a cairn. He stopped and stood upright. No, cairns were for the dead. He remembered something he'd read about the Inuit. They built *inukshuk*. Men of stone. Rocks carefully balanced one on another to a height of three feet or more, which from a distance looked like living figures. Not cairns, which were shelters for the dead, *inukshuk* were intended as company in the vast Arctic loneliness for the living, a reminder that others had passed this way, a waypost should their builder return. Temporary as flesh, permanent as stone. Dan built an *inukshuk*, balancing the large rocks as securely as he could. Would it be toppled by the wind's fury in the winter ahead? By the floodwaters of spring ice-out? Would it still be there next September to greet him? Would he be there to see it?

He turned and headed for the boat that would start his long journey home, looking back over his shoulder once at the now-tiny figure atop the island.

Author's note: The burial cairn, the sandy clearing, the large boulder with the smooth, flat rock on top, and the large ring of small fractured rocks are real. I have seen them. So is the scrub spruce next to the boulder. At that latitude the growing season for trees is very short. A tree the size of a man might be one hundred years old. The tree in the story is likely centuries old.

IV

FRIENDS GONE TOO SOON

JACK VOSS

Jack was one of my best friends. We seemed to view the natural world, and the people living in it, through similar eyes. We were both willing to undergo hardships to obtain the best and purest experiences in the outdoors, and as a consequence our shared adventures were of an extraordinarily high quality. In fact, they were a highlight of both our lives. We had a trip planned for next week to Sugarloaf Key and another in August to the Canadian subarctic.

He was a complete outdoorsman. He was tough, skilled, and ahead of the curve in the latest science and technology, and he had an abiding appreciation for the literature and art of the natural world. Every Christmas I would get a jewel of a book from him by some writer I hadn't even known existed. Shortly thereafter, I would find myself going out and buying every word the guy ever wrote.

Jack was also a great raconteur and tremendous company. He made the hours together in a car or plane pass quickly, and his stories in the evening to the assembled group of a hunting or fishing camp were absorbing and often riotous. I never gave up trying to get him to write that stuff down.

Conversations with Jack always, always returned at some point to his family. He was tremendously proud of and felt a tremendous sense of responsibility toward them, and this pride and responsibility shaped his life and made him a complete man.

He also felt a deep obligation to do right by the natural world that he loved and respected so much. He never quit leading by example in his efforts to make Atlanta Hall a demonstration of environmentally sensitive farming. Few in our community did not learn something about these techniques from watching what he did.

Roderick Haig-Brown, a fisherman and wonderfully gifted outdoor writer and philosopher, whose works were introduced to me by Jack, of course, wrote:

> If one has to die, I should think November would be the best time for it. I should think there is nothing very bad about dying, except for the people one has to leave, and the things one hasn't had time to do. When the time comes, if I know what it's all about, I suppose I shall think, among other things, of the fish I haven't caught and the places I haven't fished.

I'm certain Jack, when he knew he was going to die, thought about those uncaught fish, and unfished places, too. But a man as completely in touch with nature as Jack was had to feel also that it was wrong, all wrong, to die in the month of May—a time of rebirth, growth, and boisterous natural life. Just as it is wrong, in the natural order of things, to die leaving young children who need you. Just as it is wrong to die before your mother. Just as it is wrong to die while still so young. What was coming for Jack wasn't right at all. Yet there was no self-pity. Jack absolutely met death with his head held high. The last time we spoke, we said goodbye and then shook hands, and he looked me in the eye and his grip was strong. I will take the strength of that hand clasp with me to my own grave.

May 17, 1996

TOM VOSS

A little over 150 years ago, a Confederate cavalryman wrote these words to the mother of Frank Voss about her son, a friend and fellow trooper who had just been killed in an engagement with Union forces in Kentucky:

> He always wore high boots. I can see him as plain as if he was before me now. I shall never forget him. Many things around me are always calling him to mind. . . . I don't believe there is a day that passes by that I do not hear him spoken of. It is often the case even in one's own company that when a member of it is either killed or dies he is soon forgotten. That will never be the case with Frank, he will ever be fresh in the memory of his company and regiment. He was the most popular boy in the company—his noble character, the esteem of all, his gallantry . . . I have seen so many of our boys wounded or killed until death lost its horrors, but when Frank fell I knew I had lost more than a fellow soldier, I had lost a friend I loved with all the tenderness of a brother, a companion for eleven years, having grown from childhood to manhood together, leading each other by hand through the various paths of life . . . in which time was weaving the net of friendship tighter

and tighter around us. . . . Cruel death has separated us forever, but time can never blot out my love for him or erase it from my memory.

It struck me when I first read these words, and it strikes me now, that the apple doesn't fall far from the tree; these Voss genes are pretty darned powerful. All Tom's crustiness aside, can any of us here in this church say we ever knew a more generous human spirit?

Hearing the news of Tom's death was like a kick in the gut.

Tom endured some kicks in the gut himself. The riding prodigy Jonathan Keiser's death and that of Tom's cheerful buddy and sidekick Bob Witham are two that come to mind—both shocking and untimely.

Tom was shaken to the core, but in each case he found solace where he always did:

In the barn, with the horses he loved, particularly at night, watering off, where there were no distractions, and animal and man could talk to each other, which they did do . . .

On his beloved Atlanta Hall Farm, which he knew every inch of, on foot, maybe with a gun, or on a tractor, or in that green pickup with the cab full of condition books, Rolodexes of jocks' agents' phone numbers, and shotgun shells . . .

At home, in the drawing room, with his family and dogs, with a fire in the fireplace, watching old racing films or maybe *The Sopranos*.

And if the apple of his eye, his granddaughter Genevieve, was there with him, all the better!

Tom's professional accomplishments as a horse trainer are legion and don't need me to elaborate, except to say that when he said something about a horse or about racing, I tended to pay attention. Tom didn't deal in banalities.

I expect the Hall of Fame to come calling soon.

But all work and no play would have made Tom a dull boy, so sometimes, on the way to Colonial Downs, Tom might stop in at the Stonewall Jackson Shrine south of Fredericksburg and send me a photo of the actual bed where the great general died.

Or on the way to Far Hills Races, to stay with his dear friend Betty Merck, he would *always* stop in at Cabela's and text back a photo of something from the waterfowling section.

If the racing was at Belmont, I would often get a photo of the mural above the King Cole Bar at the St. Regis.

For a guy who didn't drink, Tom liked to *not* drink at the very best places!

This is a sad time. If there's any good in it, it's that Tom died fast and hopefully without a bit of pain. And now he can go back to Cedarhurst, Long Island, of old, with its rolling meadows, its great houses, and its legendary gentlemen jockeys.

Or he can revisit the days when the Elkridge Harford hunt country stretched from Mount Vernon Place to the Susquehanna, the land was laced in every direction with post-and-rail line fences and coverts full of foxes, and the Friday train from New York was full of ladies and gentlemen down for Saturday's meet.

And every horse had four ice-cold legs every morning . . .

January 27, 2014

PADDY NEILSON

Death smiles at all men. Only real men smile back. I've known people who were terrified of dying. Not Neilson. Tough man to the very end.

Tough jockey, too. Ebullient in victory and gracious in defeat. He didn't have to be gracious all that often. He was the dominant timber rider, amateur or professional, of our generation. He really should be in racing's Hall of Fame. Word is, though, that what's holding him back is memories of the somewhat . . . salty . . . language he sometimes directed at racing officials. Starters, in particular. Maybe when all the old farts with those bad memories have died off, he'll get his due.

Paddy had a huge heart. He never stopped wanting to make things better, whether it was the life of one individual, maybe somebody he saw falling into the abyss of alcoholism, or the lives of small groups of people—injured steeplechase jockeys—or of much larger groups of people, such as the steeplechase community, the foxhunt, or Atlantic salmon anglers. His efforts are largely responsible for prodding the National Steeplechase into a coherent program for jockey medical insurance, as well as creating a charitable fund for injured jockey supplemental aid.

There is a Triple Crown–winning trainer alive today who owes his life to Paddy.

I overheard a jockey's mother thank Paddy when the muscle-strengthening routine Paddy developed saved her son from a spinal injury.

What's going on at Fair Hill has Paddy's fingerprints on it.

There was something of the quixotic about Neilson's various and unending campaigns of betterment, and I mean that in the nicest and most complimentary way. But I was often the sounding board for his ideas in their nascent stages. More than once I had to say, "Neilson . . . promise me . . . that this notion of yours ends right here. Do *not* speak of it to anyone else!"

He and I first bonded, I guess, because we were both steeplechase jockeys and our younger brothers both raced motorcycles. But the glue of our friendship was laughter. We laughed together for almost sixty years. There was never an angry word between us. Neilson could crack anybody up. You have heard that Andy Warhol never showed or even felt any type of emotion? Well, Paddy and I were once at a party in New York at which Andy Warhol was a guest. Paddy had him rolling on the floor. I was there. I saw it. Paddy could find humor in anything; he loved the dark and ironic wrinkle. I imagine he's looking down right now and thinking with a chuckle that this is all pretty darkly ironic.

Dostoevsky wrote:

> If you wish to glimpse inside a human soul and get to know a man, don't bother analyzing his ways of being silent, of talking, of weeping, of seeing how much he is moved by noble ideas; you will get better results if you just watch him laugh. If he laughs well, he is a good man.

October 4, 2019

TRANSITION

Homewards from hunting, a December afternoon,
Thoughts turned again to a friend gone too soon.
Horses the life to which each of us born,
Only one will now hear the huntsman's horn.

The service was held a few days past,
A gathering which to my eyes seemed vast.
I'd spoken there, as friends must do
Words I hoped were honest and true,

But who can say, at such a time,
Was justice done to a soul so fine?
The anguish of his children spoke
To a parted spirit not easily evoked.

Heavy wingbeats above and behind.
My horse heard, too; didn't seem to mind.
I looked up, and just above my head
A great bird flew, continued straight ahead

In front of me, dipping low then climbing away
Higher and higher on this bleak winter day.
A bald eagle! His crown majestically white
I've seen hundreds of eagles but never such a sight.

Not perched high upon a lonely spar
Or soaring, only viewed from afar,
Fearless and nearby me he'd passed
As with some duty he'd been tasked.

I wonder if when we are gone
All that is us needs an interim home.
So much psychic energy with nowhere to go,
Could my friend be this eagle which had flown so low?

And was there here a message for me?
Was it "Thanks for your words; they fit to a T"?

ACKNOWLEDGMENTS

First and foremost, I thank Harriet Iglehart. Her fulsome praise for what I did produce over the years gave me more than enough incentive to keep going. And when I didn't write, which was most of the time, I thought I sensed, from across the rolling Maryland countryside where we both live, her quiet disappointment in me. Harriet, you're the best. This book is your doing.

Several of the pieces included here previously appeared elsewhere, some in slightly different form: "McCready Hospital" in *Chesapeake Bay Magazine*; "I'm Glad My Kids Ride" in the *Maryland Horse*; and "Idaho," "The Hay Crew," "Severe Weather," "Pond Hockey," "Messing About in April," "The Islands," "Of Weather, Sand, and Wild Places," "Varmints," "Purple Martins," "Spring Calving," "Hey, Maudie," "Cleaning the Cattle Shed," "Rockfish," "Autumn Idyll," "Willy Warner, 1980–1991," and "Cornucopia" in the *North County News*. I thank their respective publishers for granting permission to reproduce these pieces here.

Turning a manuscript into a book has been a new and eye-opening experience for me. The professionals at Girl Friday Productions made it a smooth and pleasant one. So thank you for that to book development editor Devon Fredericksen, production editor Laura Dailey, cover designer Rachel Marek, copyeditor Melody Moss, and proofreader Ramona Gault.

ABOUT THE AUTHOR

Photo © 2018 Betsy Neitzey

H. TURNEY MCKNIGHT grew up on his family's farm in Great Falls, Virginia. He attended Cornell University and the University of Michigan Law School, then moved to Harford County, Maryland, after graduating. In addition to practicing law, he rode for many years as an amateur steeplechase jockey. He also spent countless hours in small boats on the waters of the Chesapeake and its tributaries, developing a love for the beauty and bounty of this extraordinary estuary. He currently lives on his Harford County farm, and his three grown children and four grandchildren live on adjacent farms.

ABOUT THE ILLUSTRATOR

INGA CLOUGH FALTERMAN currently works as an artist in Louisiana. She received a BA from the University of Richmond in Virginia and her MFA in printmaking from Pratt Institute in Brooklyn, New York. Her current focus is large-scale representational southern landscape paintings, many of which subtly evidence the region's own conflicted directions.

Made in the USA
Middletown, DE
16 February 2021